Women
at the Well

Mini Devotionals for Women of Faith

"I know Ashley to be a woman filled with faith, wisdom and infectious positivity. This book reflects that. It's the perfect spiritual pick-me-up . . . a beautiful blend of humor and reverence. I loved it."

Jane Clayson Johnson,
Journalist & best-selling author of
Silent Souls Weeping & *I Am a Mother*

"Women at the Well is a book for all who want to strengthen their relationship and connection with God while boosting self-confidence, love, and trust. In a world that is so easy to forget God and common to feel "less than" this book awakens hope and belief in a loving, all-powerful God who knows you, loves you and is cheering you on to your greatest self. Ashley Dyer does an excellent job at sharing relatable stories and analogies in a way that is thought provoking, inspiring and spiritual nourishment for the soul."

Becky Mackintosh, author of *Love Boldly*

"The woman at the well is one of the most important stories in the scriptures. Jesus makes his first public declaration that He is the Savior of the world to this flawed but faithful woman. It is a personal invitation to each of us to have a personal relationship with Christ. He went to the woman at the well, not because she was perfect with all the boxes checked, in fact she didn't. But because her heart was open and willing. This study guide invites the reader to have an individualized time of devotion every day at your own well.

Ganel-Lyn Condie,
best-selling author/speaker/host of
Talk of Him

at the Well

Mini Devotionals for Women of Faith

by Ashley Christine Dyer

CFI
An imprint of Cedar Fort, Inc.
Springville, Utah

ISBN 13: (Paperback) 978-1-4621-4579-9
ISBN: (ebook) 978-1-4621-3157-0

Published by CFI, an imprint of Cedar Fort, Inc.
2373 W. 700 S., Suite 100, Springville, UT 84663
Distributed by Cedar Fort, Inc., www.cedarfort.com

Library of Congress Registration Number: 2023938610

Cover design by Shawnda Craig
Cover design © 2023 Cedar Fort, Inc.
Edited and typeset by Valene Wood

Printed in the United States of America

10 9 8 7 6 5 4 3 2 1

Printed on acid-free paper

To the amazing women in my life
who have knowingly and unknowingly
inspired and influenced me
in progressing towards the woman God would have me be.

And to you, _____ (insert your name here). Yes! You!
I probably can't lay claim to the title "your biggest cheerleader,"
because God snatched that up a long time ago,
but you can bet I am up there
on the list of those rooting for you. 😊

Contents

Hello, Friend!

Can I just say, thank you for showing up?! I am so excited you are here! I honestly wish we were all sitting in our comfiest clothes on the coziest couches having an unforgettable girls' night right now with yummy food and sparkling juice or hot cocoa to top it all off. But rather than watching a chick flick or getting updates on everyone's lives, like we do at most girls' nights, I imagine this girls' night to be a little bit different.

At this girls' night, we are going to go deep. We are going to get vulnerable talking about who we think we are and how that compares to who God says we are. We are going to open up about our relationship with God and all the things He has done or helped us do in our lives and what we can do to create a BFF relationship with our Creator and Maker. We are going to talk about the life lessons we've learned through the mountains we've climbed or may still be climbing and how we can hold onto hope and light in our ascent towards a more beautiful and glorious version of ourselves.

Some parts of the discussion may be hard, while others will be so so so exciting! There may be some tears—both the bad kind and the good— and there also may be some hilarious moments when we are laughing so hard our stomachs hurt. Ultimately, I hope the discussion will push us that much closer to God, ourselves, and each other, all while allowing us to have some fun together. How does that sound to you?

Now, as you have probably noticed, we aren't actually all physically together. So, I have been inspired to share my side of this deep girls' night discussion with you right here and right now, in this short devotional book. You can choose to read a chapter a day, or choose to read it whenever you need a little spiritual pick-me-up.

At the end of each chapter, I have included a little box with an invitation specifically for you based on the contents of that chapter. I hope this book gives the encouragement you need to keep being you, all while striving to take God's hand and step up to the plate of His breathtaking plan for your life. I am cheering you on big time and would obviously also love to hear your side of this deep girls' night discussion! You can reach me on Instagram at @ashley.c.dyer. My DMs are always open! So, without further ado, let's get this party started!

Much Love,

Ashley

P.S. I wrote this book while thinking specifically of women who are members of The Church of Jesus Christ of Latter-day Saints. But, for those who are not members of this church, you are still so so welcome here! Because I want to help you feel welcome, I have tried to include little notes explaining Church-specific terminology that you may not be familiar with in the footnotes. I have also tried to be clear about what books the scriptures I have included come from, as some come from the Holy Bible, while others come from the Book of Mormon and Doctrine and Covenants, which are scriptural books specific to The Church of Jesus Christ of Latter-day Saints. If you do not believe these books are scripture, that is more than ok! You can just take them as inspiring spiritual quotes. Also, just a heads up, since these are real stories from my life, some names have been changed to respect the identity of those who are a part of my story. Alright, who's ready for a party?!

Prologue

---

*"Gratitude makes sense of our past, brings peace for
today, and creates a vision for tomorrow."*
—Melody Beattie

It was 5:53 a.m., and I couldn't sleep anymore. I had woken up to go to the bathroom and by the time I got back in bed, my mind had found the "On" switch and was busy at work. I took some melatonin to try to get a bit more sleep, but it wasn't kicking in as quickly as I had hoped. Ideas were flooding my mind.

Today would be the first day of the April 2020 General Conference.[1] For the past week, in preparation for the conference, I had been pondering questions to bring with me to the meeting with the hope that I could receive answers from God. But, I was consistently drawing a blank.

Sure, I had questions. I could technically still bring all the same questions I had from last year to receive some more "in-depth revelation." But for some reason those questions seemed kind of shallow and irrelevant to me right now.

Then, the day before the conference, I finally came up with one question for God that reached my standard. It was very simple but overarching, and it seemed like the only applicable question for God right now: "What should I be proactively prioritizing and focusing on in my life

---

1. General conference is a biannual event during which leaders in The Church of Jesus Christ of Latter-day Saints share inspired messages of faith that are broadcast throughout the world.

right now to fulfill the mission and plan You have for me here on earth?" That's it. Pretty simple, right?

As I was struggling to fall asleep with my mind racing that morning, I started to receive answers to my simple inspired question, and general conference hadn't even started yet!

Definitely a first timer for me!

Funny enough, that particular week I had had a sudden prompting that I needed to be more grateful. To help accomplish this, the night before, I had started a fast. It wasn't your normal fast, during which you abstain from food and water for 24 hours while asking God for revelation, strength, comfort, or peace.

No, in the spirit of gratitude, I had been prompted to participate in a "gratitude fast." I would abstain from food and water for 24 hours and spend that time thanking God for all He had blessed me with recently. I had never heard of anyone doing this before. I wasn't asking for anything, so I wasn't expecting anything special in return. But it was what God had directed me to do, so I went with it.

As my racing mind warded sleep from my tired eyes, I finally rolled out of bed onto my knees and started having a heartfelt conversation with my Father in Heaven. I told Him about the ideas I was getting. I shared with Him my worries, fears, and struggles, and then I was prompted to write down my thoughts.

The heartwarming story of the Samaritan woman whom Jesus met at a well came to my mind. At the well, the Savior told her that those who drank from the water of the well would thirst again, but whoever drank of the water He gave—the Living Water—would never thirst again.

Suddenly, I could imagine devoted women of God coming together at a metaphorical well—not to get physical water or gossip or even just hang out, but to have faith-building conversations as they shared their "Living Water Experiences." These special experiences were the testimony-building experiences that had left them spiritually satisfied and not thirsting again.

Recently, I had been impressed that God wanted me to write a book, but I wasn't quite sure of all the specifics. Would it be written for people of all ages? Men and women? Just members of my church? Christians in general? Or for anyone?

That morning, as I continued my gratitude fast from the night before, God gave me a bucketload of information on where He wanted me to take this inspired project. He shared with me that my book would be directed toward an audience of women in the Church and be based on the memorable interactions at the well between the Samaritan woman and the Savior.

My Heavenly Father gave me a vision of women, who had had their own interactions with the Savior, coming together to share their testimonies and stories of faith. The book, He made clear, would be a devotional book in which I would share my side of the conversation—my faith-building "Living Water Experiences"—with the women of the world.

I was awestruck and dumbfounded as I looked back on all that I had written. It was only 6 o'clock in the morning! General conference wouldn't start for another six hours, yet here I was enveloped in answers to the simple question my mind had ultimately accepted after a week-long brainstorm.

Was this really happening? Or was it all a dream? Church leaders had not been joking around when they said the conference this year would be unlike any other, that's for sure! And "gratitude fasts" must be one of the most powerful and well-kept secrets of all time!

And yet, after minutes of staring down at the page now covered in what I felt were revelatory ideas, nothing changed. I didn't wake up in a daze after a really weird dream. This was real, and God's message to me was now clearer than ever. "Ashley, my sweet precious little girl," He seemed to say. "I want you to write a book for your sisters called *Women at the Well.*"

1

Lessons on a Bicycle

---

*"Trust in the Lord with all thine heart; and lean
not unto thine own understanding. In all thy ways
acknowledge him, and he shall direct thy paths."
(Proverbs 3:5–6)*

The air whipped through the bright, shiny streamers decorating the handlebars of the pretty purple bicycle I had fallen in love-at-first-sight with at a Toys "R" Us store a year or so before. As I pedaled forward, a tinge of fear caught in my throat. "Don't let go!" I yelled back at my dad who was running alongside me with his hand securely holding my bike steady so I wouldn't fall. This was going to be the biggest accomplishment of my five years of life!

My dad had driven me to the church's empty parking lot on a Saturday morning along with my adored bicycle. With me standing next to him, he had carefully unscrewed the training wheels that had acted as companions to my big white rear wheel. This was the day I was going to be a big girl—the day I would learn to balance and maneuver on my own—no training wheels necessary.

"Remember to look where you're going," my dad called out.

Why did his voice seem so far away? I quickly glanced behind me to ensure my dad's large, strong hand was still securely embracing the back of my bicycle, but before I could scream, "Help!", I swerved, and that was it. Kindergartner down!

I saw my dad running towards me as I examined my scraped knee. Before I knew it, he was at my side.

"Are you ok, Ash?" he asked.

"Why did you let go?!" my betrayed voice managed to get out as I struggled to hold back tears.

"You were doing great!" he said. "You didn't need me. You just have to remember to look where you're going. You always go where you're looking."

He quickly inspected my knee, but it wasn't bleeding. I guess he deemed I'd be fine. "Alright. Let's try again," he said with a smile.

I glowered at him. "Fine," I said. "But only if you promise you won't let go!"

"I'll be with you the entire time," he said with another smile. "You're almost there! You can do it!" He was so enthusiastic. It was kind of contagious.

I got back on my bike with an added measure of excitement and courage and soon enough, I was off again. I concentrated on looking where I was going, and I was definitely doing fairly well until it came time for me to turn.

Although I continued to look where I was going, my bicycle began tilting to one side, and logically, all I could think of doing to counter it was to lean the other way, which apparently was the wrong decision. Before I knew it, I was back on the ground with a bruised elbow. My dad ran up behind me. So much for promising to "be with me the entire time!"

"Are you okay?" he asked again.

"You let go again!" I said scowling, pointing out the obvious.

He inspected the bruised elbow and then looked at me, "When you turn, you have to lean into the turn. It might seem kind of scary at first, but you won't fall. I promise. It will actually help you turn more smoothly."

There were so many weird rules to riding a bicycle! Who had made these up?!

"Come on!" my dad said with another contagious smile. "Let's try one more time! Before you know it, you'll be a pro!"

It was hard to stay mad at my dad. "Okay," I said as I mounted my bike one last time. "But don't let go this time!"

I pushed off again and pedaled forward, making sure I was looking ahead. I cautiously prepared myself to lean into the upcoming turn and surprised myself when I experienced first-hand what my dad had been trying to explain. Turning *was* a lot smoother when I didn't try to resist and actually embraced leaning in the direction my bicycle was tilting. I tried again on the other side. I didn't fall! Amazing! I pedaled even faster, concentrating on the exhilaration of suddenly being able to travel so speedily and the wind cooling me down in the warm summer sun. This was so much fun!

Then all of a sudden from off in the distance, I heard my dad yelling, "You're doing it, Ash! All by yourself!" I turned my bicycle towards him, beaming as I pedaled now faster than ever to get back to him. He had let go again. Typical Dad. But this time I wasn't mad. My five-year-old mind was finally able to comprehend his wisdom in allowing me to go on by myself under his watchful eye. I'm not sure I ever told him, but in my heart, I remember thinking, "Thank you for letting go."

Looking back on this experience, I believe there is more to be learned from it than the basic rules of how to ride a bike. I think this can also be compared to how following God works.

First, we always go where we're looking. We can only follow God when we're looking at Him and what He wants for us. Our focus needs to be on Him and His plan rather than all the distracting things going on around us or whether or not His Hand is still holding our bicycle steady. Those distractions can just end up leaving us with a scraped-up knee and Him trying to remind us to keep our eyes on the true prize.

Second, we have to lean into the turn. At times, our all-knowing Father in Heaven places turns on our metaphorical bicycle trails. Our natural instinct is often to resist them, or lean the other way, for fear we will fall if we let ourselves move where our "bicycle" is taking us. These turns could be big life-changing events or the lack thereof, or they could be small spiritual promptings we receive.

If we follow our natural inclination to counter the turn because it is scary or uncomfortable, or even because it's not the direction we ourselves want to go, we may end up down on the ground with a bruised elbow. At this point, we can count on our loving Father in Heaven running to our side to remind us that we have to lean into the turn of His plan for us.

Although leaning in might seem kind of scary at first, we won't fall. That's a promise. It will actually help us turn more smoothly. He doesn't want us to miss out on the joyous ride He has prepared for us, complete with the wind blowing through our hair on a warm summer day as the sun shines down through the clouds and the birds chirp from the trees. "I'll be with you the entire time," He'll say with a smile. "You're almost there! You can do it! Come on! Let's try one more time! Before you know it, you'll be a pro!"

Last but not least, I want to address our constant plea to God to "don't let go!" There are definitely times when God is up close and personal, grasping onto our bicycles to steady them when they are wobbling back and forth. But, at other times He may find it more appropriate to allow us to go ahead on our own. With a loving push, He helps us start and then lets us go free. He knows that holding on will hinder rather than encourage our progress and our ability to achieve great things on our own under His watchful eye.

Now, don't get me wrong. He will never abandon us. He'll be there to yell out guidance and direction from a distance and to check on us each time we fall to make sure we're okay. But, sometimes He allows us to try out the trail independently. Although that may at times lead to small falls, those falls can be necessary learning moments. When we react by glowering at Him with a betrayed look on our face, His simple response will be like that of my earthly father: "You were doing great! You didn't need me. But here are some pointers to help prevent that from happening again."

The falls on my bicycle that day taught me important lessons I was able to use to master the art of riding a two-wheeler. Although there were scrapes and bruises involved, they ultimately led to my euphoric ride of glory at the end of the day as my sweet dad yelled from a distance, in a voice of utter excitement and joy for me and my accomplishment, "You're doing it, Ash! All by yourself!"

It will be at that point that our young minds will finally be able to comprehend the wisdom of God in allowing us to go on by ourselves under His watchful eye. It will be at that point that we can turn to Him and say, "Thank you for letting go."

Today, I invite you to reexamine where you are looking and what direction you're going. Are your eyes on the Lord and His plan for you, or are they getting caught up in the distractions so prevalent in our day? Are you embracing the "turns" the Lord has placed in your life, or resisting them due to fear or discomfort? Are you comfortable going ahead on the trail with God lovingly watching from a distance, or do you feel like God has metaphorically "let go" of your bicycle? After careful evaluation, set some goals that will help you progress on your "two-wheeler mastering" mission and place deeper trust in God and His plan for you. And, as you push off, full speed ahead, think of the contagious enthusiasm of your Father in Heaven as He encourages, "You're almost there! You can do it! Come on! Let's try one more time! Before you know it, you'll be a pro!"

2

Best Friends with God

"Greater love hath no man than this, than a man
lay down his life for his friends." (John 15:13)

On the ceiling of the Sistine Chapel in Vatican City is a fresco painting called *The Creation of Adam* by the famous Italian artist Michelangelo. This celebrated piece of artwork depicts the famous biblical story of the creation found in the book of Genesis. Aside from being a beautiful piece of art, one of my favorite Christian authors, Stephanie May Wilson, once pointed out that it can teach us a meaningful lesson about our relationship with our Father in Heaven.

In his painting, Michelangelo depicts God. His arm is outstretched, his veins are bulging, and His index finger is completely extended as far as He can manage as He tries to reach for Adam. Adam, on the other hand, is shown laying back on his side. His bent outstretched arm is resting lazily on his knee and his fingers are curled downwards as he seems to half-heartedly reach back towards God. Honestly, this kind of blows my mind.

If you saw God doing absolutely everything, exerting absolutely all He had in order to reach you, wouldn't you do everything you could to close the gap? If Adam had just straightened out his arm or his fingers in the painting, he could easily have locked hands with God. But instead he's just sitting there in a very relaxed position, looking back at God with a look that seems to say, "Can you just come a little closer? I'm comfortable where I'm at right now. I don't really want to change positions or pull a muscle by reaching any farther, you know?"

That seems like the most unbelievable thing ever, doesn't it? And yet, thinking about my own life, I feel like there have been so many times where I have been like the Adam I see in that painting, nonchalantly asking God to come closer or answer my prayers—the sooner the better.

You know those times in life when God seems super distant or a little too far away? The times when you start noticing that you haven't had as many spiritual experiences recently and you don't really feel God's presence radiating in your life? Maybe you don't even feel like studying the scriptures or saying prayers as much as you usually do. I like to call these periods spiritual lows, and, if we're being completely honest here, I think we all experience them every once in a while.

During my spiritual lows, it's always a challenge for me to figure out how to draw closer to my Heavenly Father so I can see Him, hear Him, and feel Him more intimately and more consistently. During these periods, it can sometimes be easy to feel alone or even abandoned by God. But this just isn't the case, because God has not moved an inch. He is always there with His arm fully extended, veins bulging, muscles fully contracted, and finger outstretched trying to reach us. We are the ones that have moved.

It was during one of these spiritual lows in my young adulthood that I realized that, although I knew that God was my Father in Heaven, the Creator of the world, and the Almighty and Omnipotent God of the Universe, this just wasn't enough for me. I wanted the God I worshipped to not only be the God of Abraham, Isaac, and Jacob, but to be the God of Ashley Dyer. I wanted Him to be the best friend I could talk to about literally anything—the good, the bad, and all the stuff in between.

I wanted to share my goals, concerns, and fears with Him. I wanted to tell Him about the amazing things I experienced and the lessons I learned. I wanted to talk with Him about my friends, family, and acquaintances; my dating and professional life; and my mind and my body—all the things that I could go to my best friends for. So I decided to make some changes. I decided to treat God as not only my Heavenly Father but as my Best Heavenly Friend.

I began to have more informal conversations with Him as I drove to work, the grocery store, or wherever else I was going. I took the opportunity to speak aloud with my eyes open, ditching the fancy "Thee's and Thou's" for some more casual colloquial language and telling Him about what was going on and what I was making of life, sharing my trials, fears, plans, and goals and then asking Him for advice.

I bought a prayer journal with deep prompts that helped me pour out my heart to my new Best Friend as I wrote out my thoughts and prayers and then read them aloud to Him. My prayers seemed that much more meaningful to me because I had taken the time to ponder prior to praying. I learned that God is there for us, no matter what, but we need to show Him we really want His constant, consistent presence in our lives by doing our best to draw closer to Him and asking Him to stay close to us as well.

Have you ever been in a friendship that you feel is a little bit unbalanced? Where you may feel like you are the one putting in all the effort to give time, support, listening ears, words of affirmation and validation, and gifts to brighten their days, and in return you don't exactly get all that much? I definitely have, and I must say, it is actually pretty frustrating.

I wonder if this is how God feels when He gives His all to help us get through the dark shadows and storm clouds that rain on our parade of life while, in return, we just sit back and ask Him to hurry up and make the storm end already. And, while He's at it, give us some of "Blessing A" and a little more of "Blessing B." I hate to say this, but here's a little wake-up call—this is just not how friendship is supposed to work.

Friends trust each other. They communicate with each other when things are off and do all they can to save and build the relationship they have. They are there to support and sustain each other through difficulties and challenges, to cheer for and encourage each other in brave endeavors and in achieving dreams, and to be there to listen and validate in pain and in heartache. Friends know they can count on each other. They love each other no matter what and balance each other out.

Obviously, our friendship with God will never be perfectly balanced, because He is perfect, and we are not. However, I believe it means the world when He watches us giving our all to build a relationship with Him, just as He has given His all to build a relationship with us.

The first time I wrote in one of my prayer journals, my prayer prompt was simple— "God, please be close." As I took that simple statement and began to pray to my Heavenly Father and my now Best Heavenly Friend, I poured out my heart to Him:

God, please be close. Please be close as I embark on this journey to fulfill all the dreams, goals, and aspirations You have placed in my heart. I understand You have a plan for me—an amazing plan that I agreed to in coming to Earth, a miraculous plan with aspects I probably wouldn't even believe if I was told right now. But I have faith in You and in this plan You have for me. My issue is at times it's hard for me to have faith in myself, and that is why I need You close.

I need You close guiding and directing me, comforting and encouraging me and helping me get up every time I fall, because boy am I clumsy! And boy do I know that I will probably fall over half a billion times on this journey of life! I need You there to whisper the answers in my ear every once in a while (if that's allowed, of course), to redirect me and help me realize my mistakes, to open the good doors and close the bad, and to help me find those I'm meant to find. I need You to walk with me through the storms of life, to be my illuminating flashlight as I trudge through the mists of darkness, to help me find my way back to the strait and narrow path of Your plan when I have gotten lost amongst the highly advertised detours, and to carry me when I am too tired and exhausted to take another step.

I need You by my side to protect me from the tactics of the adversary as he persistently tries to bring me down, to help me heal when I have been hurt, to listen when no one else understands, to give me pep talks when I feel weak and inadequate, and to provide me with relief when I feel like I can't go on. I need You close because I know that despite my flaws, mistakes, and imperfections, You believe in me. You are rooting for me, betting on me, working in me, and doing all in Your power to help me be the me I promised to be. You are reaching out to take my hand to guide me through the obstacle course of life that would be straight up impossible without You. And although many doubt, give up, think it's too hard or not worth it, I am not one of them.

I will keep going. I will keep moving, walking, jogging, crawling, running, and enduring to the end because I know that the further I go, the closer I get to You, to arriving on your doorstep—probably appearing quite disheveled, worn, exhausted, drained, and out of breath, with sweat dripping down my cheeks. But none of that will matter, because I will have made it. I will have made it back home to the warm embrace of my Heavenly Father and Mother[1] who love me more than all the universes combined. I don't want to give up on this joyous vision of our reunion, so please be close to help me hold on to that hope and never let go. I love You and Mother so much and I love the Savior You sent for me more than I can express. His perfect example guides my daily life and helps me understand who You would have me be. So, God, please be close. In the name of Jesus Christ, Amen.

My prayer for God to be close was actually more of a prayer that He would help me stay close to Him. It was a prayer that He would help me replace my lazy, laid-back efforts to connect with Him with the enthusiasm and strength to move a little closer, reach a little farther, and dig a little deeper. It was a petition to help me close the gap between Him and me so I could feel His warm presence as His hand locked with mine.

Recently, I started ending each prayer with an "air hug" to my Father in Heaven, and honestly it's not *just* an air hug. I grab a special pillow that I've dedicated just for this occasion and hug it hard. I imagine hugging my sweet Father in Heaven and imagine His warm embrace as I close my eyes and connect with Him at the end of each heartfelt prayer in my bedroom. Although there is an unimaginable physical distance between us, these sweet pillow hugs make all the difference in helping me feel that much closer and connected to the God I love.

Maybe hugs aren't your thing. I'm a big hugger, but I understand that not everyone is. Maybe you love music or artwork or journaling or the outdoors. Whatever you love, I encourage you to get creative. Explore what you love to share with friends and loved ones and what helps you feel that much more connected with them. Then try to implement these simple things into your relationship with your God, your Creator, and your Best Heavenly Friend.

You could start a conversation with Him with some music—play Him a song on the piano or find a track that invites the Spirit and just listen to it as you try to connect with heaven. You could draw a picture

---

1. Yes, I do believe I have both a Heavenly Father and a Heavenly Mother, because I was created in the image of God and, in my opinion, men and women don't exactly have the same image.

of Him while reflecting on who He is to you. You could write Him a letter, because who doesn't love letters? Then read it to Him in a special spot in your house, at church, or outdoors—wherever you feel most connected to Him.

The name "Immanuel," which is one of God's names, literally means "God with us." We are never alone. Even when life seems scary, we have a hand to squeeze. Even when life seems dark, we have a constant source of light to illuminate the way. Even when life seems hard, we have a Friend by our side to wipe our tears, give us an encouraging smile, and say, "I know this is tough, but I believe in you, and I'll be with you every step of the way." God is with us always—on the days we're begging to hear His voice and on the days when we don't think twice about Him, He is there—an all-loving, all-accepting, all-ears Best Heavenly Friend—the God of Abraham, Isaac, Jacob, Ashley Dyer, and you.

Today, I invite you to say a prayer and ask God to be close. Forget about all the fancy "Thee's" and "Thou's" for once and talk to God as if He were your best friend. Tell Him what's going on and what you're making of life. Tell Him your trials and fears, and your plans and goals. Ask Him for advice. Share with Him the good, the bad, and all the stuff in between. Talk with Him about your dreams, concerns, and fears; your friends, family, and acquaintances; your romantic and professional life; your mind and body; and the amazing experiences you've had and the recent lessons you've learned—all the things that you could ideally go to your best friends for. Then, you just might want to end your prayer with a sweet "Air Hug" and close your eyes as you squeeze a pillow or stuffed animal you have super tight in an effort to connect with your now Best Heavenly Friend.

3

Point of No Return

"And if men come unto me, I will show unto them their weakness. I give unto men weakness that they may be humble; and my grace is sufficient for all men that humble themselves before me; for if they humble themselves before me, and have faith in me, then will I make weak things become strong unto them." (Ether 12:27)[1]

There's a period of my childhood that I don't remember. I don't know how much of it I actually recall and how much I remember from rereading all of my journal entries from that time. All I can conclude is that period of my life is fuzzy for me. My seizures started at the age of ten, but we had no idea what they were because they presented almost like panic attacks—no funny shaking limbs or passing out, just complete fear and panic washing over me at random times. But life went on, and my family and I didn't think much of it.

Then one day, when I was 12 years old, everything changed. It was like waking up one day in a foggy atmosphere, not knowing how I had gotten there or what had happened. I was in and out of hospitals. People

---

1. Book of Mormon

told me I had fallen down the stairs at school and hit my head. I had fallen out of my chair while taking an exam and gotten a concussion. I had fallen walking down the hall in our apartment building and broken my nose. I had fallen and hit my head against the corner of a cabinet at home and somehow managed to pass out in bed.

I forgot what my friend's names were or who they were altogether. I didn't know who my teachers were or what subjects they taught. I didn't know where my school locker was and it would be useless if I found it as I would have had no idea what the combination was. There was even a day when I did not recognize my own brother. You know those moments in movies and books where something happens that leaves both the characters and audience feeling absolutely hopeless that things could ever get better? The moments where it seems like all is lost to the main characters and nothing could ever happen that would help the characters return back to either the happy place they were at before or the happy direction they were heading?

I have fondly dubbed these moments "Point of No Return" moments. I'm talking about the scene in *Finding Nemo*, when Nemo gets kidnapped by the dentist diver; in *Mulan*, when the army finds out she's a woman; and in *The Lion King*, when Mufasa dies and Simba runs away. But the funny thing is, despite all of these moments, somehow in these stories and movies, something happens that causes everything to somehow work out in the end, just maybe not the way the protagonist imagined it would. You may say, "Well, that only happens in movies!" But, I beg to differ.

One of my favorite quotes is: "If you could see the story God is writing in your life, you'd never be jealous of anyone else's."[2] We are co-authors with God of our own stories, and sometimes He allows unexpected plot-twists to be thrown in.

For me, this "fuzzy period" of my life was one of those times. It was not only a "Point of No Return" plot-twist for me, but for my family as well. My parents were absolutely devastated as they watched their once cheerful, smart little girl, who was always anxious to try new things and prove herself to the world, become a tired, wounded, desperate soldier with amnesia, trying to push her way through the haze now surrounding her.

---

2. Stephanie May Wilson

These "Point of No Return" moments seem absolutely horrible when they hit. But actually, when you look back at them, you realize that they are rightly called "Point of No Return moments" because of the game changer they play in pushing these characters to the next level of growth, at which point there's no going back to what was once "normal," as normal has just upped its game.

These plot twists may seem absolutely horrendous in the moment, but they ultimately push the characters to problem-solve, seek support, find courage, and achieve things they never imagined they could have ever done before. It is not "in spite of" these moments that the characters push through and achieve great things, but "because of" them.

In *Finding Nemo*, losing Nemo pushes Marlin to overcome his fear of the ocean and allows Nemo to recognize how strong he is even with a gimpy fin. In *Mulan*, the discovery of Mulan's true gender pushes Captain Shang to recognize her great commitment and spare her life. This in turn allows her to be in the right place at the right time to see that the Huns are still alive and then warn the emperor and save China. In *The Lion King*, Mufasa's death and Simba's escape pushes Simba to find a support system in animals he never would have hung with before. These unique friendships allow him to learn, grow, and gain new perspectives so that when the time comes for him to return to Pride Rock, he is stronger than ever before and can take his rightful place as king.

For me, experiencing this new, scary challenge pushed me to search for God and cling to Him for dear life wherever I found Him. It pushed me to find comfort in knowing I had a Savior who knew exactly what I was going through and who knew exactly how to help me. With God by my side, this trial pushed me to do everything in my power to one-up this obstacle and show it who was boss. I was able to work with God to co-author how we wanted to use this plot-twist to make my story that much more exciting and my character that much more capable.

Another one of my favorite quotes, is by Dieter F. Uchtdorf:

For a moment, think back about your favorite fairy tale. In that story the main character . . . must overcome adversity. . . . You will experience your own adversity. . . . It is your reaction to adversity, not the adversity itself, that determines how your life's story will develop. . . . Your own wondrous story has already begun. Your "once upon a time" is now.[3]

For some reason, looking back at the foggy memories of that particular "Point of No Return" moment in my life, I recognize that in that difficult and scary time, as I clung to my Heavenly Father and Savior as my go-to support system, They blessed me with peace. They blessed me with the courage to sweep the question "Why?" into the dustpan and instead pick up the question "What?"—"What is this for?" "What does this mean for me?" "What should I do with this 'Point of No Return' moment?"

Maybe I was so tired, forgetful, and desperate at the time that I didn't even want to mess with "why," because I knew it wouldn't exactly get me any answers that would satisfy. Now, looking back though, I can confidently say I have discovered the *why* by searching for the *what.*

This "Point of No Return" moment was a game-changer for my life and pushed me to learn and grow in spirituality and resilience. It helped me gain an unbreakable testimony of God's love for me, as I clutched His Hand tightly so He could lead me through the mist. It helped me develop resilience, courage, and confidence in my ability to do hard things, to overcome challenges, and to get back up each time I was pushed to the ground.

Without that life-changing moment, who I am today would be levels of mediocrity below who I am now. So, although it was hard at the time, looking back at how far I've come, I can only lift my eyes to heaven and thank my God for blessing my life with that difficult, scary "Point of No Return."

And oh, how my heart longs to reach out to that helpless, confused, forgetful little girl in the fog and say, "Hey you! I know this is tough! Like really tough! But I also know you are strong! Like really strong! Believe me, I know! And I promise you that even though this fuzzy time in your life is going to be hard and confusing and tiring and make you want to cry sometimes, someday you're going to be glad it happened."

And that little girl will lift her eyebrows at me and say, "What are you talking about?!" And I will answer, "I'm talking about the strong person you are going to become, the hard things you are going to have

---

3. Dieter F. Uchtdorf, "Your Happily Ever After," April 2010 General Conference, churchofjesuschrist.org.

the courage to do, and the people you are going to be able to lift. I know it's hard to understand right now, but stay strong! God has plans for you that are so great you wouldn't believe them even if I told you. Trust me! 'If you could see the story God is writing in your life, you'd never be jealous of anyone else's.' So although this is rough, I promise from the bottom of my heart, it will be worth it."

Then with big, outstretched arms, I will give that young, naïve little girl a ginormous bear hug and a huge bar of chocolate and will do anything I can to make her laugh, because laughter is good for the soul, right?

How are we reacting to adversity right now? Are we cowering in fear and hopelessness at the "Point of No Return" moments in our lives? Or are we trying to stay positive and still find ways to do good and fill ourselves with hope that we can spread through our communities, states, nation, and world? Are we asking, "Why is this happening to me?" or "What would God have me do with this?" Because, as Elder Uchtdorf said, "It is [our] reaction to adversity, not the adversity itself, that determines how [our] life's story will develop."

How are you today? Are you doing fairly well? Or are you maybe finding yourself at one of those "Point of No Return" moments and could use some encouragement? Today, I want you to look back at your life. Find a "Point of No Return" moment in your life, and discover the why in the what. Recognize how hard it was for you, but also recognize why it was worth it.

Then send a message back to your cute, struggling self back in that moment. Tell her you know it's hard but someday she will be glad it happened. Give her the words of encouragement she needs so she can find the courage, resilience, faith, and hope to keep pushing through. Tell her how worth it it is going to be.

If you find yourself at one of those plot-twisting moments today, write a letter to yourself from your future self with those same words of encouragement. You may even want to give yourself a ginormous bear hug and a huge bar of chocolate and do anything you can to make yourself laugh, because laughter is good for the soul, right?

4

Fearfully and Wonderfully Made

---

*"None of us came to earth to gain our worth; we
brought it with us."* — *Sheri L. Dew*

I am so inspired by the concept of our divine nature and potential as
children of God. It is a unique belief that sets us apart from other
faiths. Yet the Bible clearly implies our divine inheritance:

> *The Spirit itself beareth witness with our spirit, that we are the
> children of God.*
>
> *And if children, then heirs; heirs of God, and joint-heirs with
> Christ; if so be that we suffer with him, that we may be also glorified
> together.*[1]

So why is it that if the Holy Bible itself declares the validity of this
doctrine, we as humans are so hesitant to accept it? I honestly think it is
because of a rampant pandemic of insecurity and a failure to truly recognize one's individual worth and potential. The adversary has done so well
at encircling us with demeaning, debilitating, and destructive messages.

---

1. Romans 8:16–17

He's even gotten us to produce those messages in our own minds and get them to play on repeat—"I'll never be good enough," "I'm so stupid," "I'm an absolute failure," "I'm unworthy of anything good," "I'm too ugly, too dumb, too fat, too bad, too prideful, too extra, too dirty, too un-Christ-like."

Yuck! Those are the most demeaning, vulgar, toxic, cruel things someone could say about you! Yet somehow, Satan has tricked us into incorporating them in our internal monologue. How did that even happen?! The saddest thing is that it's generally not a once in a while thing. It typically doesn't happen just once a month or once a week even. It can happen on a daily or even hourly basis.

I absolutely hate when the word "too" is put in front of a word with a negative connotation and used to describe a child of God. I hate when people complain they are not "good enough," "pretty enough," "smart enough," or "strong enough." But I find myself doing this in my own poor, worn-out brain more times than I can count. So how can we over-come this?

I remember one day back in high school, I was riding the bus home after school and a guy I didn't know very well called me a very vulgar name. I was shocked. No one had ever called me that before, but I chose not to respond. I didn't want to make a big scene and ignored him. I knew what he said wasn't true, so I was fine just brushing it off.

My little brother, on the other hand, was absolutely furious! "Say that again, and I'll punch you!" he said, staring this older boy down with the boldness and courage of a lion being challenged by an overly prideful hyena.

I don't remember what happened next. All I remember is being stunned and overwhelmed by the strong expression of love my brother, the little boy I fought with incessantly, had just demonstrated as he flew to my defense when someone attacked me.

This experience makes me wonder how our Beloved Brother and Savior Jesus Christ would respond when He hears someone verbally and emotionally attacking us, including our own selves. His love for us is so great that whenever anyone treats us cruelly or disrespectfully, He has taken it upon Himself to suffer alongside us.

Our loving Heavenly Parents begot us as well. They are our Flawless Creators and Makers. How do you think they feel and respond when we are attacked by others or ourselves? I can't imagine they would just sit back and watch, completely unfazed by what just went down. Our Heavenly Family are our greatest Supporters, our most enthusiastic Cheerleaders, and our strongest Advocates. Seeing us torn down must upset them more than we can imagine. It may make them want to immediately fly to our defense with a desperate yet bold plea of, "Please don't talk about my sister or daughter that way!"

In Psalms 139 it says:

I will praise thee; for I am fearfully and wonderfully made: marvellous are thy works; and that my soul knoweth right well.

My substance was not hid from thee, when I was made in secret . . .

Thine eyes did see my substance, yet being unperfect; and in thy book all my members were written, which in continuance were fashioned when as yet there was none of them.[2]

I love this scripture, as it describes the process of our creation. It describes our loving Heavenly Father fashioning all the "members," or parts, of our body and seeing our "substance"—the important characteristics we would have. Though not perfect yet, these elements would be essential in helping us achieve our divine potential.

Our substance was not hidden from Him. He was fully aware of our imperfections. Yet not a single thing about us was a mistake, because guess what? God does not make mistakes. God does not make stupid. God does not make ugly. We were "fearfully and wonderfully made"—made by a Creator in whom we should fear, or respect, and stand in awe of at the wonders of His creations.

The Psalm goes on to say:

How precious also are thy thoughts unto me, O God! How great is the sum of them! If I should count them, they are more in number than the sand.[3]

This scripture that directly follows the description of our creation, really touches me. I have reflected on how my God would respond each time I insult the imperfect body, character, or identity He has gifted me.

2. Psalms 139:14–16
3. Psalms 139:17–18

I have considered how He would sorrow as He suffered alongside me in my overly demeaned mind. I have imagined the frustration He would feel as I repeatedly attacked myself and He repeatedly tried to come to my defense, attempting to be my Advocate and Healer.

It is hard to realize that my Heavenly Father has attempted to share how He truly feels about me, but in my anguish I have been unable to comprehend the messages He is trying to send. *"How precious also are thy thoughts unto me, O God! How great is the sum of them! If I should count them, they are more in number than the sand."*

How does it make you feel to know that your loving Father in Heaven is continuously trying to send you precious messages that are uncountable? Are we so stuck in our own heads, giving in to the temptations of a mean jealous enemy to bag on ourselves over and over again that we cannot recognize the "marvellous" creation we are and the "marvellous" potential we have? If the adversary's tactics cause us to think twice when someone tells us about our "divine nature and eternal destiny," it looks like something has to change ASAP!

My dad taught me from a young age how to respond to criticism. "First," he would say, "You can ask yourself if it's true. If it isn't, you need think nothing more of it. If it is, you can decide what you want to change so you can improve yourself." Those words of wisdom from father to daughter have stuck with me over the years.

I recognize though that sometimes being our own worst critics doesn't help so much when carrying out this task. So the next time that voice in your head starts tearing you down, I want you to pause and say a small prayer, asking your greatest Supporter, Cheerleader, and Advocate if whatever was said is true. Then listen for the "precious thoughts" that come. If you hear something along the lines of, "Please don't talk about my sister or daughter that way!", please think nothing more of it. If it is true, together with your Loving Maker, decide what you want to change so you can improve yourself, and always remember you are "fearfully and wonderfully made."

Over my bed, I have arranged a bunch of colorful sticky notes to form the shape of a big, gigantic heart. On each of these notes I have written, in sparkly silver or gold sharpie ink, the "substance" God has given me—who God knows I am and the characteristics God knows I have. I found each of the words to put on these sticky notes by combing through the scriptures and searching for testimonies of how God sees me.

These sticky notes include strong, bold words like "VALIANT," "PRECIOUS," "DAUGHTER," "CHOSEN," and "ENOUGH." Behind each of the sticky notes, I have written scriptural references to support my claims. Today I want to invite you to do a scriptural search for who you are to your Loving Heavenly Father. Write down your findings and place them somewhere you can see, somewhere you won't forget, somewhere that will be easily accessible when the adversary tries to tempt you to turn on his pre-recorded radio track of cruel, demeaning, self-deprecating comments in your head.

Here's some scriptures to help you get a head start, but don't limit yourself to just these!

The Holy Bible:
> *Matthew 5:45; 7:11*
> *Ecclesiastes 3:11*
> *Proverbs 8:32; John 20:29*
> *Matthew 5:16*
> *Isaiah 13:12; 43:4*
> *John 15:13–14*
> *Galatians 5:1*
> *1 Corinthians 7:20*
> *Jeremiah 31:3; Malachi 1:2; John 3:16*
> *Mark 4:38; Luke 10:34*
> *Matthew 11:28–30*
> *1 Chronicles 19:13; Joshua 1:6*
> *Joshua 1:9; 2 Corinthians 12:10; 2 Timothy 2:1*

Latter-day Saint Scriptures:
  Alma 13:3
  2 Nephi 26:30; D&C 4:5
  Mosiah 5:7; D&C 76:24
  Ether 12:27
  2 Nephi 1:15; 4:21
  2 Nephi 23:12
  D&C 4:3

5

The Scriptures Aren't Boring!

"And now, my [daughters], I would that ye should remember to search [the scriptures] diligently, that ye may profit thereby." (Mosiah 1:7)[1]

I have definitely gone through phases of my life when the scriptures seem very intimidating—old books with archaic language that can just downright confuse me. They often provoke too much thought for me to handle, or they cause my brain to tell me she's decided to turn in early for the day and to try this scripture thing again tomorrow, next week, or even next month.

"But I have to read these books to be a good Christian!" I think to myself. "It's what church leaders are telling us constantly! 'Search the [scriptures] . . . every day, every day, every day!'"[2] But at that point my sweet old cerebrum has already gotten into bed and turned out the lights and I'm left to do this checkbox task on my own with absolutely no support from her at all.

I remember one day, not too long ago, I was really struggling with my scripture studies. After 12-hour shifts at the hospital, I would come home

---

1. Book of Mormon
2. Kevin W. Pearson, "Stay by the Tree," April 2015 General Conference, churchofjesuschrist.org.

completely drained of energy, get showered and cleaned up, and find myself sitting on my bed with my scriptures open and my head drooping. I would try to keep my eyes open as I read a chapter before drifting off to sleep. There were more times than I can count that I "fell asleep at the wheel" and would wake up unsure of what verse I had left off on.

This continued for far too long, until one day I put my foot down and said, "Okay. This has to stop! If scripture study is supposed to be so good for you that the church leaders keep urging me to do it every day, every day, every day, I've got to be doing something wrong!

"Everyone talks about feasting upon the words of Christ, but I'm consuming it like I consume one of those disgusting mini cups of cherry cough syrup that leave me gagging and grabbing a cup of water to wash down the grossness and relieve my poor offended tongue. So, yeah! Something is obviously wrong! We've got a problem here, and it's about time I solve it!"

After my heated statement-to-self, I was more than committed to starting my detective work to solve this mysterious, confusing dilemma. The problem was, I had no idea how. So I did the only thing I could think of and went to my Almighty, All-Knowing, All-Loving, All-Powerful Creator and Maker to ask for some help.

"Heavenly Father," I said. "As You know, I'm really struggling with this scripture study thing and don't know what to do. Can You help me appreciate the scriptures more? Can You help me learn to feast upon the words of Christ?"

Each day, I repeated this prayer, asking for some more much-needed help and support. And each day that I did this, I noticed a difference. "Help me notice one new thing that intrigues me and stands out to me today so I can learn more and expand my understanding of You," I would pray. These quiet, innocent, humble, genuine prayers seemed to be much more powerful than I expected because almost every day that I offered them and invited God into my scripture study, I would learn something new about Him.

Next, I decided that I needed to set the perfect stage for my scripture study, with the perfect place, the perfect time, and the perfect props. Scripture study was going to be a morning thing for me now. Not a last minute, last hurrah of the day, try-to-keep-your-eyes-open type of task. It was not easy, because I am definitely more of a night owl than an early bird, but I wanted to show God I was willing to make a sacrifice to put Him first. I was going to put "Word before world."[3] I was going to invest my time and energy in this book before I touched my phone in the morning, before I checked my texts or emails or Facebook messages, or before I headed out to work. Word before world! It's something I have to remind myself pretty much every day.

I invested in a beautiful journal-edition of the scriptures—one I knew would put a smile on my face each time I took it out to read because of how pretty it looked. I also selected a beautiful pink floral journal out of my unused journal collection—one I knew I would be excited to write in with my pretty pink Pentel Energel pen.

I purchased some colorful pens to write down my insights and draw pictures that would make me happy to look back on, reminding me of what I had read or learned about that day. I also bought a daily devotional book to start off my scripture study each day and a prayer journal to help me connect with God on the days when scripture study seemed more difficult.

I then set to work each day trying to better understand my God and how He works in my life. I worked to comprehend how the scriptures mean so much more than a boring check-the- box, complete-the-assignment task to so many people. I tried to fathom why the prophets of old included these specific things in these books and not something else.

With these proactive changes, I suddenly began to have meaningful insights as I searched for answers within the book that I had once deemed old, archaic, and too hard to comprehend. I became intrigued by words that stuck out to me this time around that I once had been confident I knew the meanings of, but now wasn't quite so sure. "What does the word 'luster' actually mean? What about the word 'tender?' Or 'dealings?' Or the word 'fortify?'" And the definitions surprised me. I had been ignorant of these things before I was all-in committed to understanding more, to understanding better.

God began helping me nerd out in a book that had once made me yawn. I started looking up topics like "water" and "vipers" to see why the prophets of old had used these terms metaphorically. My findings brought so much added insight and awareness into what God had been

---

3. Gretchen Saffles

trying to communicate to me all along. It was a transformative experience watching the once "dull" words turn into such desirable "food for thought" that I couldn't wait to gulf down another serving as I woke up each morning.

When I was really struggling, I called up my best friend, told her I was having a hard time with meaningful scripture study, and asked if she would be my "Scripture Study Buddy." She enthusiastically agreed as she was struggling as well. It figures! We began reading the scriptures together in funny voices, making dramatic comments, asking each other questions, trying to come up with answers, and just having the time of our lives. It was absolutely wonderful!

In this way, God converted my brain from a tired, lazy, indifferent character, who was often too hasty to excuse herself from the once less-than-desirable task of opening that big old book that sat near my bed, to an awake, excited, invested persona, keen on learning that much more about the God she loved. I was absolutely mesmerized about what had come from the effort I had put into saying those humble prayers for help. I was so proud of myself for doing all I could to find the goodness in this familiar task that had once seemed intimidating, boring, and absolutely annoying. Now it seemed like a readily available, intriguing, exciting, and soul-filling blessing from God.

Just like that, I learned that the scriptures are the most insightful, magical collection of books ever to touch the face of the earth. If we put in a little extra effort and ask God for some guidance, support, help, and direction, we will learn that these books are "Treasure troves of truth," "Diamonds in the rough," and "Pearls of great price." We will learn that the scriptures are anything but boring!

How are you doing these days with your scripture studies? You can be honest. No judgment whatsoever coming from me no matter what you say! I promise! If you're at a spiritual high and feasting on the Word like I gulf down nacho fries at Taco Bell, then I can't tell you how happy I am for you! Keep up the good work! You got this! And do everything you can to not lose it! You've found the precious gift that so many others are striving to find in their lives.

Now, on the other hand, if anyone feels like I once did with the scriptures sometimes tasting like gross cherry cough syrup and seeming too archaic, confusing, intimidating, and boring, can I just reassure you that you are so not alone! Believe me! I've been there! And so many other people are struggling too! So no shame! No blame! No judgment! Nada! I am so here for you! The fact that you recognize the struggle and are maybe wanting to change things up to find this "Gift of feasting" says loads about your character!

So if you are in that place right now, I want to invite you to switch things up a little. Before your next scripture study, I want to invite you to say a genuine prayer. Ask God to help you learn to feast on His word. Ask Him to help you find something new and intriguing, something that will catch your attention and spark some thought, something that will help you learn a little bit more about who He is and what He does as you attempt to feast on His word today.

I also invite you to consider your scripture study stage. Is there anything about the time, place, and props you use for your scripture study that has maybe made it less successful than it could be. If so, I invite you to experiment with different places, times, and props until you find the perfect stage for you.

Next, find opportunities to nerd out in your scripture study. Look up words you come across in the scriptures that might help you better understand the truth they have to offer. And finally, if all else fails, reach out to a friend of choice and ask them if they will be your "Scripture Study Buddy."

I hope this helps and can't wait to hear how it goes!

6

"Kaphar"

"*For according to the great plan of the Eternal God there must be an atonement made, or else all mankind must unavoidably perish.*" (Alma 34:9)[1]

During my last semester of college, I had a pretty traumatic experience. It was early in the morning as I was driving to the hospital for a clinical shift as a nursing student. I was driving in a construction zone on the highway, but it was so dark outside that I did not notice any of the construction warning signs and was going the normal speed limit. Before I knew it, there were flashing lights behind me. I was on the left side of the highway and I had never been pulled over by a cop before, so I instinctively just pulled over to the farthest lane to the left and stopped.

The officer came running over and banged on my window, which I rolled down nervously. "Are you trying to kill us?!" he yelled and then directed me to move to the right side of the road. I was quite shocked and the nerves in my stomach didn't help as I tried to follow his instructions as efficiently as I could. I started heading to the opposite side of the highway from a standstill but it was really hard for me to see behind

---

1. Book of Mormon

me because of the flashing lights. As I pulled over to merge into the next lane, all of a sudden something big hit me.

My car swerved perpendicular to the road upon impact and everything sort of happened in slow motion. I saw my life flash before my eyes and all I could think in that instant was, "This could be really bad."

I ended up crashing into the concrete median in the middle of the highway. The airbags released, but I don't think I hit them. I just had a mild headache from whiplash and my knees hurt a bit after colliding into the dashboard. I was in shock for a while, but I was okay.

I remember my initial feelings following the accident were shock, disbelief, and a little bit of anger. I remember thinking, "Heavenly Father. Why did this happen? This morning when I said my morning prayer, I specifically prayed that I would do no harm to anyone and that no one would do any harm to me. I prayed I would be able to drive safely. How could you let this happen?" Then I sort of forgot about that thought as I was swept into the chaos.

When I eventually looked over at the car that had hit me, I was surprised to see it was a gigantic semi-truck that I later found out was taking a number of hot tubs to Alberta, Canada. The driver was alright aside from what looked like some broken bones in his hand. He said he was grateful I was ok. My boyfriend at the time came to pick me up and, after the officer was done with me and gave me a speeding ticket (Yeah. For real!), he took me to the emergency room.

My vitals were stable and, upon assessment, the doctor told me I was looking good and he didn't think radiation would be worth it for imaging. We then drove home and I tried to get some rest but the accident kept replaying itself in my mind, making sleep impossible. It was then that the question "why" popped back into my head as I again reflected on my morning prayers.

I was so angry, frustrated, and confused. Then, as I sat there ruminating on all these negative emotions, I suddenly had an epiphany as I realized that in all actuality, my Heavenly Father *had* answered my prayer. I had come out of that accident practically unscathed with nothing more than a small headache and some bruised knees, and the truck driver had come out with only a couple broken fingers. I mean, how many people come out of a semi-truck accident without having to be rushed in an ambulance to the hospital? Or alive, for that matter?

That truck driver and I coming out of that accident with such minor injuries was an answer to my prayer. It should have been a lot worse. We should have come out with much more major injuries. We could easily have died. But Heavenly Father heard my prayer and answered it.

At that moment, I suddenly felt overwhelmed by the love of God. It was as if He was telling me, "Ashley. I love you infinitely. Now was not your time. There are so many more blessings I have in store for you during your mortal ministry, so many more lessons I would have you learn, and so many more lives I would have you bless. Your mortal mission is not over yet." As I realized this, the tears I had been holding back all day finally came and I broke down crying.

In Hebrew, the word for atonement is *kaphar*, which means "to cover." This experience helped me realize that God has got me covered— not just my transgressions, but my accidents, my fears, my mistakes, and my struggles. He knew that in my morning prayers I would pray for safety. He knew I wouldn't notice the construction zone signs. He knew there would be a cop that would pull me over. He knew I would pull to the wrong side of the road. He knew that the cop's flashing lights would make it difficult for me to see my blind spot. He knew that semi-truck and I would collide. He knew I would come out with nothing but a headache and some bruised knees and the other driver with nothing but some broken bones. He knew my boyfriend would be willing to pick me up at the scene at 6:30 a.m. on a Sunday morning. He knew. He knew I would feel anger and confusion. But He knew it wasn't my time to go yet. He knew He still needed me on earth, and He knew He could help me understand. He knew. He had me covered.

I went to Church that afternoon and got up to share my testimony. I still remember the first words I spoke into the microphone, "I wasn't supposed to be here today, but it seems like God had other plans for me." I recounted all that had happened that morning and broke down crying as I related the message of love the Lord had sent me in an effort to communicate to my ward[2] members that I hoped they didn't need to have near-death experiences to know that God loved them infinitely as well, that there were so many more blessings He had in store for them, so many more lessons He would have them learn, so many more lives He

---

2. "Ward" is another word for "congregation."

would have them bless, and that they too were still needed in this mortal ministry. Now was not their time to go either, because just like me, God had them covered and would have them covered for the entirety of their lives through His great atoning sacrifice—the precious *kaphar* I was able to appreciate that much more because of everything that happened that day. I could now trust that no matter how difficult or scary or frustrating or sad life got, God had me covered.

In times of hardship, sometimes it seems like the last thing we want to do is recognize God in our lives. Sometimes it hurts to realize that God is letting not so great things happen to us. After all, He is our loving Heavenly Father. But I want you to take the time today to recognize that God loves you infinitely. The fact that you're alive today means there are so many more blessings God has in store for you during your mortal ministry, so many more lessons He would have you learn, and so many more lives He would have you bless. Your mortal mission is not over yet. And though it may include times of challenge and difficulty and times when it is hard to understand why things happen the way they do, know that through it all God knows. He knows you. He knows what you need. He knows what you can handle. And He has got you covered. Take a moment today to reflect on how you've seen kaphar in your life, or instances where despite hardship, it was clear looking back that God knew you and all you were going through and had you covered.

7

Horrible Plant Mom

"The Lord loves effort, because effort brings rewards
that can't come without it." – Russell M. Nelson

Just like I've never been good at keeping goldfish alive for over a time period I would rather not admit, I've also never been good at keeping plants alive. As much as I'd like to think I am a caring, responsible individual (I mean, I *am* a nurse for goodness sake), being a plant mom is not my forte.

One day, post-college, I bought three small, cute cacti and succulent-like plants that I found at an outdoor market in the park. I affectionately named them Priscilla, Gwendalyn, and Isabelle and sat them on the windowsill in my kitchen. I would spray them with water whenever I remembered, which probably isn't the greatest way to care for plants if we're being honest.

But soon enough, I noticed that Priscilla didn't look so good. I tried to be more diligent at watering the trio of sisters, but in the next week or so, Isabelle had begun to wilt as well. They all looked a bit more shriveled than they should be. I was just a tad bit embarrassed. As a grown adult, how was I so horrible at taking care of three small cacti? I mean these things survived on their own in the desert, right?

Soon enough, Priscilla and Isabelle had passed. I put green candles in each of their small pots to try to make them look like purposeful decorations. They were kind of cute, but looking at those tiny pots that sat on either side of the now semi-shriveled Gwendalyn—which my roommate claimed she had mistook for dead when she repotted a plant of her own and took the tiny stones that decorated Gwendalyn's base, I was absolutely ashamed! Can anyone else relate? Or is it just me?

I mean, I thought plants were so pretty and having plants in the home made me feel grown up, responsible, and naturalistic even. But how many plants was I going to go through before any of them lasted? Should I just deem myself an irresponsible plant mom and give up or follow the age-old proverb, "If at first you don't succeed, try, try again"? I decided to go with the proverb.

One day, while passing through Home Depot, I spotted some cute succulents. I definitely thought twice about purchasing them, but ultimately decided that I wanted to show myself I could do hard things! So I bought two small succulents and laid them in another sunlit window in my house. This time I was determined to succeed! I did a Google search on succulents and how often I should water them and up popped some watering and fertilizing tips from the Cactus and Succulent Society of San José. That sounded official enough, right?

I read, "While growing, cacti and succulents should be watered at least once a week. Some people water more often than this. During each watering, give the soil a good soaking, so that water runs out of the 'drainage holes' of the pots."

Well, that new knowledge definitely brought on a bit of embarrassment. All I had been doing with the three beautiful baby triplets was squirting them every once in a while with a spray bottle, which now that I think about it, the plants probably found almost taunting. "Here, have a drop of water or two every once in a while and it will relieve your dehydration!" Yeah. That warrants a full-on bright red blush and downcast head from me—the plant teaser and horrible plant mom.

With this newfound knowledge I decided to be better and show these new plants some much-needed love. Every Sunday I would soak them through with water, and on the days in between, I would give them a few squirts every now and then, just in case they might be extra thirsty.

And, aside from one brown leaf that shriveled up a little on one of them, they seemed to be thriving.

Then one day, a few months later, someone made a comment at church that really hit home with me. "I'm trying to take care of plants," this one girl said, "but it isn't easy," she continued. "I've found that if I wait until the plant tells me it's not doing well, it generally dies; whereas if I proactively look up what the plant needs and follow the directions, it will survive." Whoa! Talk about familiar!

Thinking back to that comment, I actually don't remember why she said that or how it related to the discussion we were having. But I honestly think this is kind of how it works when it comes to caring for ourselves and our spiritual well-being. I mean, think about it. Our wonderful Father in Heaven has given us a lot of direction when it comes to how to best achieve happiness in this life and the life to come. We can get this direction from the commandments; the scriptures; the apostles, prophets, and other church leaders; the whisperings of the Spirit; the personal revelation; and more. Yet for some reason, although this direction is readily available to us, sometimes our stubborn, imperfect selves don't put in the effort to search, listen, read, and follow as diligently as we should.

We think to ourselves that someday we'll get around to it, or we'll be fine without it for a day or so, or "that doesn't really apply to me." It's only once we recognize we have become so distant from God—so unhappy inside, so needful of the Lord's presence in our lives—that we think to take action, decide to look up some much-needed directions, or decide to proactively care for the shriveled leaves and withering water-deprived roots. And by then, it's a little too late for an easy fix. It will require a lot more effort on our part to water our roots adequately to get back to the spiritual thriving point we are hoping for.

Honestly, it all kind of comes down to the pride cycle. We become really close to God at times, and then our pride causes us to get just a tad bit complacent to the point at which we feel like we don't need to put in so much effort. Then we get distant and realize we actually do need to be a bit more proactive in seeking God's presence in our lives, and the cycle continues.

Our Lord and Savior Jesus Christ is the Living Water. As He told the woman at the well, "Whosoever drinketh of the water that I shall give

[them] shall never thirst; but the water that I shall give [them] shall be in [them] a well of water springing up into everlasting life."[1]

Rather than dehydrating our spiritually thirsty selves with the wrong kind of watering methods, let's go to the Source of Living Water Himself for direction and guidance on how to help our spirits flourish and on how to prevent any withering roots, browning leaves, wilting stems, or straight-up candle memorials. Let's not wait until our spirits tell us we aren't doing so well and instead proactively look up what we need and do our part to follow the easily accessible directions to help our spirits survive and even thrive.

Now, I understand that this is a lot easier said than done. And just like I'm a horrible plant and goldfish mom, sometimes I'm not the most caring, responsible nurturer of my spirit either. But the good news is, God is also a Supporter and Enthusiast of that age-old proverb that I used as an excuse to buy some more plants following the devastating demise of my old ones. I believe He, hands down, will repeatedly and consistently encourage us in our spiritually distant sorrow: "My sweet daughter, boy do I have some water to fill your soul, and I promise it's worth the effort, so try, try again if at first you don't succeed, because my beautiful girl, you can do hard things.

Take some time to ponder your spiritual well-being today. Are you feeling up close and personal with your Heavenly Father right now? Or maybe a tad spiritually distant? Are you spiritually hydrated? Or spiritually dehydrated to a point that warrants a full-on bright red blush and downcast head? Wherever you are, I feel you. And God feels you too. He feels you in your spiritual happiness and in your spiritual sorrow. He feels you in your blossoming spiritual self and your withering one as well. So wherever you may be, let's focus on filling our soul with the rehydrating living water the gospel offers and keep in the back of our minds the encouraging spiritual pep talk, "If at first you don't succeed, try, try again."

---

1. John 4:13–14

8

The Man Born Blind

"Yea, I know that I am nothing; as to my strength I am weak; therefore I will not boast of myself, but I will boast of my God, for in his strength I can do all things." (Alma 26:12)[1]

In college, I had the opportunity to go on a four-month study abroad in Israel. It was an unforgettable experience. After walking the city streets in Jerusalem, interacting and bartering with the locals of different cultures and backgrounds, and visiting some of the world-renowned biblical sites, I came home better able to imagine what it was like for the people of Christ's day to live in the Holy Land.

While there, I fell in love with the story of the man born blind, who Jesus declared was born this way not because he or his parents had sinned, "but that the works of God should be made manifest in him."[2] This short, miraculous account came alive in my mind one day as I sat pondering the man's healing experience after visiting the sacred pool where he regained his sight.

---

1. Book of Mormon
2. John 9:3

In the story, Jesus makes clay of spittle and dirt and anoints the eyes of the blind man and then tells him to go wash in the Pool of Siloam. Immediately, this short-of-sight man gets up and goes for it, then soon afterwards, comes back with his vision restored. When the Pharisees ask him who has healed him, he replies by saying that he honestly doesn't know but that whoever it is must be a prophet.

Well, obviously they don't like that answer, so they go and ask this man's parents, who basically respond with, "Yes. Our son was blind and now he can see. We don't know how. Why don't you ask him? He's a grown man. He can tell you the whole story."

As the Pharisees continue to press this man for more information, hinting that Jesus is a sinner, he finally replies by saying, to put it simply, "I don't know if he's a sinner or not. All I know is that I was blind and now, because of Him, I can see. Why are you so upset because of this marvelous thing? Why are you so mad because my eyes are opened? I believe in God and do my best to do His will, and now He has heard my prayers. If this man were not of God, He could do nothing."

Later, after the Pharisees cast this man out for testifying that he knows his Healer is of God, Christ comes to him and asks him if he believes in the Son of God. His meek response touches my heart, "Who is he, Lord, that I might believe on him?"[3] When Christ ultimately reveals His true identity, the healed man immediately responds by proclaiming, "Lord, I believe"[4] and worships him.

After living in Jerusalem and walking around and outside of the Old City near the Pool of Siloam, I quickly observed that wherever you go, the pathways are not smooth and straight. There are hills and steps and cobblestones and rocks as well as constant turns and thin trails. There are large crowds of people pushing against or through you on a mission to get from one place to another. I imagine it would have been similar back then. I don't know where the blind man was when Christ anointed his eyes and sent him to the Pool of Siloam, but I am impressed that this man who could not see was so willing to make the journey to this pool after Christ sent him there.

---

3. John 9:36
4. John 9:38

In the Bible, there are many examples of people not accepting invitations to be healed. Naaman the leper initially resisted the Prophet Elijah's command to go wash in the River Jordan and be healed. The children of Israel even resisted looking at the brazen serpent to be healed of their sickness. However, this faithful man, who could not even see where he was going or see who had told him to go there, immediately got up and made the journey to the pool where he had been directed to go.

I can only imagine this man holding onto the stone walls on the sides of the street, walking carefully up and down stairs so as not to lose his footing. I picture him crying out to ask for directions from anyone who could hear him, pleading to know if he was anywhere near his intended destination. I see him being constantly bumped into and pushed forwards and backwards by the oncoming crowd as he sets forth on this mission to get from wherever he was to the pool Christ had indicated. It could not have been an easy journey, and yet his response was immediate, and his decision was rewarded. And now, he had the most amazing adventure story to tell anyone who would lend a listening ear. It's funny how that works, isn't it?

This story is one of great faith. This innocent, humble man, who had been blind since the day he was born had probably wondered what the different textures he had felt with his hands were. He may have heard about beautiful scenes and colors that he had longed his whole life to see. Perhaps, he had the desire to know if he looked anything like the two people who cared for him and called him their son. He was willing to do anything to achieve this. His condition had refined and humbled him and made him a prime candidate for the blessings of the Lord. The Lord's commandment to wash in the Pool of Siloam gave him hope that he never had before and that hope quickly became faith that he acted upon. This man may have been "short-of-sight" physically speaking, but his response to the unexpected invitation to be made whole showed the depth of his spiritual vision.

All of us have challenges in our lives—some may be physical, others mental or emotional, and others spiritual. But I believe these challenges are generally not given to us because we are bad people. And, even if they are brought about by our own decisions, I believe that ultimately we are given challenges so that the works of God can be made manifest in our lives if we but have faith.

In the scriptures, we are invited to "come unto Christ, and be perfected in him, and deny [ourselves] of all ungodliness; and if [we] shall deny [ourselves] of all ungodliness, and love God with all [our] might, mind, and strength, then is his grace sufficient for [us], that by his grace [we] may be perfect in Christ; and if by the grace of God [we] are perfect in Christ, [we] can in nowise deny the power of God."[5]

The man born blind was willing to put his trust in the Savior and come unto Him by obeying His commandment. His love of God and act of faith allowed him to access the Lord's grace and he was healed. The works of God were made manifest in his life and he could not deny God's power even when he was harassed afterwards.

This story illustrates that when we love and trust the Lord and obey His commandments, although we may be imperfect, His grace will be sufficient and we will be able to see His Hand in our lives. This does not necessarily mean that God will take away our challenges, but because of the Atonement of Jesus Christ, He will always know how to succor us in our trials when we turn to Him for help.

Dallin H. Oaks once said, "Healing blessings come in many ways, each suited to our individual needs, as known to Him who loves us best. Sometimes a 'healing' cures our illness or lifts our burden. But sometimes we are 'healed' by being given strength or understanding or patience to bear the burdens placed upon us."[6]

How often do we feel like this blind man, trying to follow God and feel our way through the twists and turns of the rocky trail of life as we call out for help and directions, trying not to trip on the jagged rocks we can't see? How often do we find ourselves trying to ultimately beat the odds and get back to our heavenly home as we attempt to show our faith in God and try our best to do His will, praying for help along the way? Is it just me that struggles with this?

Well, guess what? I've got some good news. God did not send us to earth with a curt, "May the odds be ever in your favor!" Because, honestly, it's not about luck being on your side. Instead, I imagine our Heavenly Family whispering in our ear right before our mortal journey began, "Remember, when you partner with God, the odds are always in

---

5. Moroni 10:32, Book of Mormon
6. Dallin H. Oaks, "He Heals the Heavy Laden," October 2006 General Conference, churchofjesu-schrist.org.

your favor," as They sent us into mortality to learn of their grace, their love, their faith, and their sacrifice.

I love the words of the traditional Christian hymn "Amazing Grace" that I feel could easily be sung by the blind man who made the journey of faith to the healing waters of Christ.

Amazing grace! How sweet the sound
That saved a wretch like me.
I once was lost, but now am found,
Was blind but now I see.

This wretch, or unfortunate blind man, was lost in darkness when he was found by the Savior who offered him His saving grace and provided him with not only his restored sight but with the eternal vision of the gospel so that the odds would forever be in his favor. I know that no matter our life situation, we are forever favored by our loving Father in Heaven. Though at times we may feel lost, our all-knowing, all-loving, and all-powerful God will always win in a game of Hide-and-Seek; He will manifest His works and power in our lives if we have faith; and He will give us the most amazing adventure stories to tell anyone who will lend a listening ear. It's funny how that works, isn't it?

I feel like all of us can relate to the blind man in certain ways. Maybe we feel like we're going through a dark or rough time; maybe we feel lost, maybe we feel like we're trying to blindly find our way to wherever we're supposed to be and could use a helping hand; or maybe we've experienced healing in ways we've been praying for for ages. Whatever it may be, let's take some time to ponder how we've seen the sweet grace of God in our lives recently. Remember, when you partner with God, the odds are always in your favor. Today I invite you to ask yourself how you can better partner with God so that the works of God can be made manifest in your life.

9

A Bag Full of Stones

"Forgiveness is not an occasional act; it is a constant attitude."—Martin Luther King

---

Have you ever struggled to forgive someone? Maybe it's just me, but I definitely have. Every once in a while, someone does or says something or I make a realization about all this pain I have because of the things someone has done, maybe even unintentionally. I often find myself weighed down by this big burden of negative emotions towards that someone (at times that someone could even be myself). Then, as a large negative cherry on top, I feel guilty about feeling all of those negative emotions, because I need to be more Christlike and just let it go and forgive already.

When this happens, I get to this place where I feel kind of stuck—part of me wants to stew in those heated emotions, while another part wants to run as fast as I can in any other direction and escape at all costs. However, running away is always a little harder than expected because the heated emotions are like quicksand dragging me down, and it's up to me to find something to grab onto so I can pull myself out and not get buried alive. It's clearly an emotional mess.

There was one point in my life when I was caught in this horrendous place. I'd been there before, with the same negative emotions towards the same person, and I was feeling pretty crummy for being unable to get past it all, so I did the only thing I could think of: I decided to ring up my Father in Heaven and ask for some help and advice to figure out this whole "forgiveness" thing and how it really worked, because it didn't seem to be working out so well for me at that moment.

Then one night soon after, I had a dream. In my dream, I was hiking up a mountain. Now, I love hiking! So, it didn't seem like anything out of the ordinary. As I was walking, I suddenly noticed that the backpack I was carrying was kind of heavy, so I took it off and looked inside. You'll never believe what I found!

In that large bag that would have hopefully been filled with snacks or water or a jacket or first aid kit, was nothing but rocks! Like, for real?! I was so confused! Why on earth would I be carrying a bag of rocks? Was this some type of weird resistance training or something?!

I took each of those large stones out one by one and tossed them on the ground. Then I zipped the bag back up and, with the empty bag on my back, I started hiking again. The scenery was beautiful. I tried to soak up the nature and the fresh air as I walked until suddenly, I stopped dead in my tracks. My bag was starting to feel heavier again. I quickly tore it off and looked inside. Well, you can imagine my horror when I opened it up again and found it filled with another assortment of stones. Was I going crazy?! Was someone punking me?! What on earth was going on?! I was getting frustrated. I quickly poured the rocks out on the side of the trail, zipped the bag, and started hiking again.

But this time, rather than just walking along like nothing had happened, I went into stealth mode. Every few steps, I would look behind me, and that's when I saw them. These same pesky rocks were following me and trying to sneakily jump in my bag when they thought no one was looking. (Remember, this was a dream.) But still, I was downright angry now! I tried to block the rocks with my hands. I tried to run away. I tried to do everything I could to prevent them from carrying out their evil scheme, and it worked to an extent, but every so often, my efforts would be in vain, and another rock would make it in. They were like magnets, and apparently for some reason I was super magnetic. This was going to be a rough hike and not because of the altitude or terrain.

As I continued to walk, I noticed that I became more adept at this new game of dodgeball, because every time I checked my bag and emptied it out, there were fewer rocks inside. That cheered me up a little bit. At least I was making some progress. I began to enjoy the views and pay more attention to the beauty of God's creations. It was nice.

Near the top of the mountain, I stopped again to check my bag. What was my surprise when I found only one small rock inside. It made me smile to see how far I had come in my pest-control endeavors. This was such a strange, yet funny experience. Then finally, when I got to the top of the mountain, I checked my bag one last time. To my surprise, there was nothing in it. Not a single pebble. I felt so much lighter. It was beautiful.

When I woke up that morning, that dream was still vivid in my memory. As I reflected on it, I began to find meaning in the curious narrative. I realized that those rocks represented far more than pests or small annoyances. They actually symbolized the grudges I held against those I struggled to forgive. As I said my prayers and repented of those grudges, it allowed me to relieve the burden of those rocks in my backpack. Yet, generally it wasn't just a one-time thing that would allow me to get rid of the burden in the long run. Those rocks would come back, chasing me like magnets, and I would have to continuously repeat the process.

At first, it would be frustrating and at times make me feel weak and even angry at my inability to get rid of those rocks with the snap of a finger. But over time, as I continuously said those prayers of repentance, asking for help in my forgiving endeavors, it got easier. Little by little, try by try, and prayer by prayer, it would become that much easier for me to throw out the rocks, or the grudges I held against those who I felt had wronged me, and keep them out.

In the story of the woman caught in adultery, the woman's accusers anxiously ask the Lord if He agrees that they should stone her as commanded in the Law of Moses. Jesus's famous response to those seeking to justify withholding forgiveness is, "He that is without sin among you, let him first cast a stone at her."[1]

What are we doing with the stones in our lives? Because I feel like every time we hold onto grudges, we collect another stone to cast in our mind, another stone to weigh down our metaphorical backpacks on our journeys of life. When in reality, God has given us full permission to empty our bags of stones and leave them at His feet on the trail

---

1. John 8:7

beside us. This does not mean that they won't try to sneak back into our bags, because forgiveness is a process, not a one-time event. Persistence is key to mastering this gift as we consistently check our "backpacks" each day and empty them of rocks. But as we work at it, those stones will decrease in size and magnitude and be easier to avoid on our trail-blazing adventures.

How is your "backpack" feeling these days? Are stones, or grudges, weighing you down? Is there someone in particular you are having a hard time forgiving? Remember, that someone could even be yourself at times. Right now, I want you to take those grudges and lay them at the feet of the Savior. Lighten your load today. And if they come back tomorrow, just do it again. And again and again and again. Forgiveness is funny, because it can be quite the long-lived process, but I promise, practice makes perfect and, with time, it will be worth it.

10

Keeper of the Gate

"Behold, I stand at the door, and knock: if any
[woman] hear my voice, and open the door, I will
come in to [her], and will sup with [her], and [her]
with me." (Revelation 3:20)

I can still remember my first Christmas as a missionary.[1] I was visa-waiting in the Tennessee Nashville Mission and serving in a small town out in the boonies populated by a large elderly population. I had two awesome companions named Sister Leavens and Sister Jones. For Christmas Eve dinner we had Ritz and Triscuit crackers with ham and cheese, French bread with oil and vinegar, and apple slices with Sister Jones's homemade brown sugar cream cheese dip—not exactly a feast, but it's what we put together.

I remember waking up with my companions, excited to see what our families had sent us in the presents we had tucked safely under our mini, artificial Christmas tree that we had fondly named Evangeline. As we opened our presents, Sister Leavens and I discovered that we had both received a small gift from Sister Jones's family. After opening them, we

---

1. At the age of 20, I set aside a year and a half of my life to share the gospel of Jesus Christ as a full-time volunteer missionary for The Church of Jesus Christ of Latter-day Saints in Nashville, TN and Natal, Brazil.

found that our companion's mother had sent each of us a cute necklace adorned with a large silver key.

"My mom gave these out at church," Sister Jones explained. "You know how in that painting of Christ standing at a door and knocking,[2] there is no doorknob? Well this key is just a reminder that we have the power to open that door and allow the Savior in."

For some reason that hit me deeply. I had never noticed that the door in that well-known painting by Del Parson did not have a door-knob on the outside. Nor had I thought much about the power the Lord had entrusted us with to open the door to Him when He stood outside knocking and waiting at the doors of our hearts. It was actually kind of mesmerizing to me.

I wore that necklace a lot throughout my mission as a reminder of my responsibility to allow Christ into my life each day. Sometimes members would tease me when they saw it, asking who had given me "the key to my heart." I would respond with the meaningful story of that first Christmas on my mission. I had the key to my heart. I was the keeper of the gate, and it was up to me to unlock and open it to those I desired to abide with me, especially my Savior Jesus Christ.

When I returned home from my mission a year later, I made friends with a cute girl at church who was preparing to be baptized. One day, her mom came up to me and told me that she had asked her daughter who she would like to speak at her baptism. Her daughter immediately chose me. I was flattered and set to work praying and asking God what I should speak about. His clear-cut response was that I should speak about doors. "Doors?" I thought to myself. And then it hit me, and I eventually got it.

On the day of my sweet little friend's baptism, I did in fact talk about doors. I related the story of my silver key-shaped necklace and spoke about ways to open the door to the Savior each day. I talked about praying, reading the scriptures, going to Church, and partaking of the sacrament.[3] I explained how each time we did these things we were open-ing the door to Christ and allowing Him to enter our lives and abide with us. We were inviting Him to fill our lives with light and love unlike any other.

---

2. "Jesus at the Door (Jesus Knocking at the Door)," painting by Del Parson.
3. Every Sunday, members of The Church of Jesus Christ of Latter-day Saints partake of bread and water to remember the promises they have made to follow God.

I then told her that another set of doors she would be able to open in the future would be the doors of the temple[4]—God's house, where she would be able to make even more promises with Him, do His work, and get married for eternity. I urged her to always live a good and obedient life so she could make it through those doors and to tell all the boys who chased after her that "if this isn't your castle, then you aren't my prince," because God had a bright and brilliant life prepared for her as long as she was willing to open the door and invite Him in. She was the keeper of the gate and God had entrusted her with the key just as He had for each and every single one of us.

When I left the mission field, I gave that large key-shaped necklace to a convert. Recently, I was given another necklace with a mini key dangling on the end. On it, in small letters is engraved the word "Believe." Not only does it remind me of the responsibility God has given me as a keeper of the gate to my life and my heart, but it also stands as a reminder that I can believe in myself and my capacity and diligence to open that door and not let a single day go by without doing so. God stands waiting for me, just a twist of a doorknob away, and I will not pass up the opportunity to feel His intimate presence in my life each and every day He blesses me with.

---

4. Members of The Church of Jesus Christ of Latter-day Saints go to special buildings called temples to make promises with God and get married and sealed together for eternity.

How is your relationship with your Savior today? Are you experiencing His intimate presence in your life? Or could things be better? What are you doing to open the door and allow Him in to abide in your heart every day? Is there more you could do as the keeper of the gate? Maybe you need to work on some of the simple things like prayer, scripture study, and sabbath day observance, or maybe you have to go a little deeper and try things like fasting, getting a priesthood blessing, going to the temple, or preparing to receive a patriarchal blessing.[5] I think we all have something we could work on a little bit more. Today I want to invite you to get on your knees and pray. Thank your Father in Heaven for the many times He has shown up in your life and then ask Him what more you can do to open the door and gate more persistently and consistently so that the Savior can enter and fill your life with His light and love.

---

5. Priesthood holders in The Church of Jesus Christ of Latter-day Saints can give blessings with inspired messages from God. The temple is a sacred place we go to make promises with God and get married for eternity.

53

11

Wilt Thou Be Made Whole?

---

*"But Jesus turned him about, and when he saw her,
he said, Daughter, be of good comfort; thy faith hath
made thee whole. And the woman was made whole
from that hour." (Matthew 9:22)*

During my scripture study one day, I was studying in John 5, which recounts the story of Christ healing an invalid, or impotent, man on the Sabbath. The dictionary definition of the word *invalid* is "a person made weak or disabled by illness or injury," and the definition of *impotent* is "unable to take effective action; helpless or powerless."[1]

I had read this story multiple times in the past, but the one thing that stuck out to me this time was that it was Christ who actually initiated the healing process by asking the impotent man, "Wilt thou be made whole?"[2] In the majority of the biblical healing accounts, I feel like it is generally either those who have deficits or their family or friends that go to Christ to seek healing. However, in this circumstance, Christ actually proactively went up to this weak, helpless, and hopeless man and asked him if he wanted to be made whole.

---

1. Definitions from *Oxford Languages*.
2. John 5:6

As I have thought about this question and event recorded in the scriptures, I have thought about those I know as well as those I have cared for as a nurse in the hospital setting who struggle with infirmities that make them "unable to take effective action," that make them "helpless or powerless," and that deplete them of hope. Some of them have faith in God and have been through adversity before, which helps them press forward during difficult times. To these individuals I have had the privilege of sharing my testimony of the blessings that come when we put our trust in God and His plan for us without giving them false hope. But, sadly, the majority either never had or no longer have this faith. It is no secret that adversity often hardens hearts. It happens to the best of us.

It makes me wonder if the impotent man Christ healed had ever seen or heard of the Savior and His miracles prior to being asked if he would be made whole. Maybe yes, maybe no. But it seems as if he had not, as he claimed he did not know who had healed him when the Jews later asked him.

Whether or not he had seen or heard of the Savior before, it is clear that this disabled man could not be healed alone. The saying was that an angel would come down and disturb the waters, and when this happened, whoever was the first person to enter the waters would be healed. The man's response to the Savior's question demonstrated his continued hopeless state, "Sir, I have no man, when the water is troubled, to put me into the pool: but while I am coming another steppeth down before me."[3]

This man was too weak to throw his disabled, frail body into the water himself—quite a daunting task that could result in further injury or even death. He knew he couldn't stand a chance competing with those individuals who were a part of the "great multitude of impotent folk, of blind, halt, withered, waiting for the moving of the water"[4] who had the ability to walk or someone to help them. It was obviously a lost cause. Yet the Savior came.

In the painting *Christ Healing the Sick at Bethesda* by Carl Bloch, Christ is depicted gently lifting up a tapestry that covers the impotent man, who is hunched up in darkness on an improvised bed by the pool.

---

3. John 5:7
4. John 5:3

He appears too discouraged and demoralized to show his face and ask for help after 38 years of fruitless waiting.[5]

As He lifts up the cloth, the Savior allows both the literal light and the light of hope to stream into this man's dark makeshift bedroom, and instructs him simply to "rise, take up (his) bed, and walk."[6] The scriptures quote the man's response, "and immediately the man was made whole, and took up his bed and walked."[7]

I love the word "immediately" in this verse. It illustrates the magnitude of hope the Savior brought to this suffering man, who found it within himself to be proactive and do the impossible because of a simple yet powerful invitation from God. As I reflect on this account, I am prompted to think about our reactions to adversity, whether that is physical, emotional, mental, or anything else for that matter.

At times it is very easy to feel weak, helpless, powerless, and alone. It is easy to feel like we are surrounded by darkness. When others ask us if we want to get better it is often tempting to say, "Well, of course, I want to get better, but there are all these things standing in my way," and sink even further down into the depths of despair and hopelessness.

Yet from this account we learn that even in the times when we do not proactively seek the Savior amidst our trials and challenges, Christ, in His love, will come to us and ask, "Wilt thou be made whole?" It is then up to us to decide how we respond. It is up to us if we will "immediately" react to His commandments and invitations that will help us become whole or ignore them and sink further down into the depths of despair.

There are a few things that are important to understand regarding how the Savior works. The first is the definition of the word "whole." Many of us can often mistake this word to mean "free from any more trials or challenges." Unfortunately, this is not the case. We live in an imperfect world. Just when we think the road is smooth and straight, we often run into a few more bumps and twists and turns. But in spite of these rough roads along our path, there is no reason we can't ask the Lord to ride shotgun.

One of my amazing mentors e-mailed me the other day with a message that I thought was really meaningful. She said:

---

5. John 5:5
6. John 5:8
7. John 5:9

God is not in the business of leaving things broken and messy. He's not a God that sees a hard situation, shrugs, and says, "I guess I'm not really sure what to do with this one!" He's a God that brings life from death, beauty from ashes, hope from despair, light from darkness, and healing from the most broken, mixed up, and messy situations. We can stand on those promises. We can lean our lives against them; we can trust Him to do those things for us.[8]

When God asks us if we will be made whole, He is not asking us if we will let Him take away all of our problems. He is asking us if we will put our trust in Him and take His hand and follow Him so He can teach us how to feel less broken, less alone, less fearful, less self-conscious, less depressed, less anxious, less hurt, and less ashamed. He is asking if He can help us feel more love, more peace, more comfort, more hope, more faith, more confidence, more healing, and more joy. He is asking if we will let Him be on our team as He says,

Come unto me, all ye that labour and are heavy laden, and I will give you rest.
   Take my yoke upon you, and learn of me; for I am meek and lowly in heart: and ye shall find rest unto your souls.
   For my yoke is easy, and my burden is light.[9]

I honestly always had a hard time understanding this scripture. How could the Savior's yoke be easy and His burden light when He suffered for all of our sins, pains, trials, and infirmities? But a couple months ago, I finally found a way to help me understand it. Rather than asking us to take His yoke upon us, I think the All-Powerful, Almighty Savior is asking if we will allow Him to help us carry our yokes.

If you know anything about yokes, they aren't meant to be carried alone. They are made to be carried by two oxen who work together to balance and pull heavy loads. At times we labor so hard with our heavy burdens that we feel stuck in the mud of life. Yet, the Savior comes and offers His helping Hand. If we consent, He will gladly help us carry our load and we will indeed find rest.

The yoke becomes so much lighter with the Almighty Light of the World there by our side to help us lift. Just as the impotent man needed

---

8. Stephanie May Wilson
9. Matthew 11:28–30

another to help him lift his burden, we need Christ to help lift our burdens as we accept His invitations and commandments and trust in His will and timing for us.

The second thing that is important to understand is the Lord's timing. This man was not healed until he had struggled with his infirmity for 38 years. I am not sure why his trials had to last so long, but I'm sure the Lord had a reason. Sometimes our trials and challenges have to last a while, maybe much longer than we think is fair or justifiable.

For me, healing is often a longer, more subtle, and more personal process than those accounts from the Bible in which we read about the Savior helping the blind to see and the deaf to hear and the lame to walk in what seems like the blink of an eye. When we are faced with periods of waiting in desperation, I think it is often better if we are proactive in seeking out the Savior and asking Him to help us heal, as many other individuals struggling with infirmities did in the biblical accounts.

Christ has said, "Draw near unto me and I will draw near unto you; seek me diligently and ye shall find me; ask, and ye shall receive; knock, and it shall be opened unto you."[10] We still may be asked to wait a little, but the Lord may give us some commandments to help us thrive and maintain hope in the process of waiting. One of those commandments may involve humbling ourselves and asking for or accepting help from family, friends, teachers, leaders,

strangers, or certified health professionals. You name it! Timothy J. Dyches once said:

> President Thomas S. Monson has said, "There is one life that sustains those who are troubled or beset with sorrow and grief—even the Lord Jesus Christ."
>
> If you feel unclean, unloved, unhappy unworthy, or unwhole, remember "all that is unfair about life can be made right through the Atonement of Jesus Christ." Have faith and patience in the Savior's timing and purposes for you. "Be not afraid, only believe."[11]

The last thing I believe is important to understand is that there is no competition when it comes to the love of the Lord. We live in a world of

---

10. Doctrine & Covenants 88:63 (Latter-day Saint modern revelation and scripture)
11. Timothy J. Dyches, "Wilt Thou Be Made Whole?" October 2013 General Conference, churchofjesuschrist.org.

competition and comparing ourselves to others, and social media definitely makes it hard for us to overcome this. Even the impotent man in Jesus's time was faced with competition as he was just one individual of a great multitude trying to be the first one in the water when it was troubled. His cry of despair was "but while I am coming, another steppeth down before me."[12]

Although this chapter only recounts the incident of Christ healing the impotent man, I have every bit of faith that he was not the only impotent individual there that Christ healed. I have every bit of confidence that Christ went on to offer healing to the multitude surrounding that pool in His own way and time.

Christ is aware of and loves each and every single one of us. He loves you. He loves your family. He loves your friends. He loves your enemies. He loves that individual on the other side of the world whose story you don't know. But He knows. He knows their name; He knows who they are; He knows their likes and dislikes; and He knows their trials, challenges, struggles, and tribulations, just as He knows yours.

There is no competition, no rivalry or race, no contest or comparison, because He will ask the same question of each and every one of us. If we so desire, we can have our own personal agenda with Him at any time, in any place, and in any situation. He is there reaching out and waiting for us to either proactively ask for help or respond to His merciful invitation just as the impotent man did that day at the pool of Bethesda.

The Lord is all-powerful, all-merciful, and all-loving, so when we feel weak, when we feel down, when we feel powerless, when we feel hopeless, or when we feel alone, we should not isolate or confine ourselves in darkness. We must be willing to ask for help. We must be willing to trust and take the Savior's extended hand and accept and act on His invitations and commandments. We must be willing to allow the Lord to be on our side and help us carry our yoke through His grace. He is there, He knows who we are, He loves us infinitely, and He is willing to help. His simple question to us is, "Wilt thou be made whole?

12. John 5:7

Is there something going on in your life right now that might be making you feel weak? Disabled? Unable to take effective action? Hopeless? Or powerless? How are you responding to this? Are you hiding behind a tapestry, hunched up in darkness, too discouraged and demoralized to ask for help? Or are you ready to step up to the plate of hope and swing your bat at whatever comes at you even when you feel like you stink at baseball?

I want to promise you that no matter how dark or hopeless life may seem at times, your loving, merciful Savior and Friend is right next to you, with a strong arm outstretched beckoning you to come unto Him and asking, "Wilt thou be made whole?" I feel like life itself is a journey to achieve wholeness. In a world where challenges are constantly beating us down and wounding our hearts, it can be a trial to even keep moving forward each day.

But the second we take the Savior's outstretched Hand and tell Him we're in, He'll respond with a smile, "Ok. But you gotta trust me. I've been down this path before and it might be kind of complicated and may take longer than you hope, but it will be worth it. I know the way. I'll be with you the entire time. You just have to stay close and trust that we're going to make it through this together."

Today I want you to metaphorically take the Savior's Hand. Tell Him you're all in, express your trials and challenges, your dreams and desires. Ask Him for help to get where He wants you to go to be made whole. Then listen. Some answers may come quickly while others may come at a slower pace. But when you receive the answers He sends your way, I hope you can have the faith of that impotent man and "immediately" take action. Partner with God to progress towards wholeness, trust His timing, and remember, there is no competition in the question, "Wilt thou be made whole?" because that question is purely personal, which means when the Savior asks, "thou" equals YOU and no one else.

12

The Cure for Loneliness

"A new commandment I give unto you, That ye love one another; as I have loved you, that ye also love one another." (John 13:34)

Loneliness is like the common cold these days. It plagues our communities, our neighborhoods, and our homes. A common misconception is that loneliness is caused by a lack of friends or company. But I can't bring myself to fully accept that when so many people who are surrounded by others claim to feel lonely. So how can we fix this? What's the cure for loneliness? That's a very good question and one God recently gave me an answer to.

I have found the cure for loneliness is love. Now, I'm not talking about romantic love or even friendship. I'm thinking of godly love—loving as the Savior would and filling your life with the presence of His love for others and yourself. I'm talking about service, self-care, and quiet time with God.

This means developing a relationship with Him that allows you to see both yourself and others through His eyes because, boy, does He love His children. We are all precious in His view and dear to His heart. When we feel alone, I bet there's nothing He wants to do more than give us a giant Daddy-daughter bear hug.

Once we start loving and developing a tighter relationship with Him who loves perfectly, that lonely void we feel will be filled and then some, so that our lives will be permeated and encircled by the enemy of loneliness itself—love.

In the Book of Mormon, the prophet Lehi said he had beheld the glory of God and was "encircled about eternally in the arms of His love."[1] So, how can we feel that heavenly embrace when loneliness plagues our lives? I think that in order to feel God's love and presence in our lives, we must take steps to love as He loves—give genuine compliments, participate in service activities, be there for someone in need, go the extra mile to make someone smile, counter negative thoughts about ourselves with words of affirmation, and take steps to better love and care for our bodies and minds.

One time I saw the effects of this was during the COVID-19 quarantine. I had two roommates at the time but that hardly meant anything as a nurse working night shifts during this highly stressful period. I remember working the Saturday night shift leading into Easter Sunday. Someone had been kind enough to leave Easter candy at the nurses' station, and Reese's mini eggs are the best! So even though I went home that morning with a tummy ache, I went home having had a taste of the fun side of Easter, which I thought I would miss completely that year.

I went back to work Sunday night, not having spent any time celebrating the holiday with my roommates. Despite the nice Easter treats, with all the craziness going on related to the coronavirus plaguing the community and hospital, I was feeling a little empty, or you could say lonely. By the time work was almost over, I was exhausted, but when I spotted some leftover up-for-grabs Easter eggs in the break room, a light switch went off in my head.

I was pretty sure my roomies hadn't had any Easter treats because of the stay-at-home order and the fact that we were all in quarantine far away from family, so I decided I wanted to change that. After sterilizing the Easter eggs (because you never know what kind of germs are hanging out at the hospital), I brought them home with the idea of setting them outside their bedrooms with some candy and a nice note inside, but on

---

1. 2 Nephi 1:15, Book of Mormon

the way home, I got a better idea. Why not put up a full-on Easter egg scavenger hunt?

Now, by the time I got home, I was so worn out and exhausted that I had second thoughts multiple times, but I knew my love levels were running low. I desperately needed to refill my tank, so ultimately I went for it. It was actually exciting putting the hunt together as my oblivious roommates were sleeping. I collected some nice goodies I could give them—candy, Chapstick, jewelry, and books—and wrote little riddles as clues for my roommates to find the next treat. Then I went about hiding the prizes and left their first clue in an envelope outside of their bedroom door.

And as I laid down to go to sleep that morning after a long night shift, I couldn't help but smile as I listened to my roommates shriek with excitement as they went about finding their hidden surprises. Love filled my heart, and I went to bed a little less lonely that day. And imagine my surprise when I woke up later that afternoon to find that one of my roommates had "heart attacked" my door as I slept, leaving sticky notes with sweet messages of love and appreciation that filled my tank that much more. Loneliness may be a plague, but a little bit of love to counter it will lead to more love, because love is contagious, and the cure for loneliness is love.

Have you or someone you know been feeling a little lonely lately? This week I want you to help refill both your tank and the tanks of those around you with love. Heart attack someone's door, give someone an exciting surprise, be there for someone in need, go the extra mile to make someone smile, talk positively to yourself, write a nice letter to someone who would appreciate it, participate in a service activity around you. I promise that as you do so, your love tank will fill to counter the loneliness that may leave you feeling a little empty, because in order to see Him who loves us best, you have to try your best to love as He loves, and the cure for loneliness is love.

13

Sturdy Brick Walls

"No pain that we suffer, no trial that we experience
is wasted." —Orson F. Whitney

Palm Sunday, the Sunday before Easter, is a day often overlooked but a day to be celebrated all the same. It was the day of Christ's triumphal entry into Jerusalem and the beginning of His last week of life. It was the day numberless people welcomed Him into their city awaiting what they thought would be a miraculous time in which the Messiah would conquer the city and free them from their current oppression.

Although the Savior certainly had the power to do all those things, He did not do them in the way that they anticipated. What Christ did was actually much more than the people realized or expected. Instead of conquering their city, He would conquer the world. Instead of freeing them from their current oppression, He would free them from all the oppression, pain, and suffering they would ever experience in their lifetime. But because He did not do exactly what they expected, they deemed Him a blasphemer and quickly lost interest and rejected Him. Yet, despite the lack of their support, He continued on to serve and liberate them in the most sacred and love-filled way anyone has ever served or liberated in all history.

These people seemed to expect and hope that many of the prophecies of the Second Coming of the Savior would occur that day—prophecies of the destruction of the wicked and the building of a New Jerusalem in which Christ Himself would rule. Although these things will surely come to pass, it was not time for that yet and there were other more important things that needed to happen first.

We all have certain expectations and hopes of God. Do we expect that He will liberate us from current oppression in a *specific* way? Because He certainly has the power to do so. Do we hope that He will grant us certain revelation on why we are going through what we are going through and how to make things happen? How many of us, like the people who rejoiced and welcomed Him warmly that Palm Sunday so long ago, find ourselves disappointed when things don't happen the way we think they will and begin to doubt or lose faith and hope in the liberating power of Christ's Atonement?

I have personally struggled with feelings like these when it comes to the expectation and hope for marriage. Growing up in the Church, I was surrounded by a culture that constantly spoke about the hopes and joys of marriage for eternity, about keeping yourself sexually pure for that eternal companion, being worthy of a celestial marriage, and bringing children into this world.

When that's talked about so much, it kind of becomes this relentless dream that you expect just has to fall into place smoothly because it's what God wants for you, right? So if you have that righteous desire and are doing all you can to keep the commandments and follow Him, why in the world would He hold out on you when it comes to that special blessing you're seeking?

I mean, I had it all planned out. Do well on the SAT, get into BYU, and soon enough that handsome, temple-worthy Prince Charming would step into my life and sweep me off my feet. It would be fate. Eternal fate. After all, that's what happens at BYU, right?[1] Everyone knows that.

Sure enough, I did well on the SAT, got into BYU, and started seeing the magic happening all around me . . . to everyone else that is. My freshman roommate met her Prince Charming during our first semester,

---

1. Brigham Young University is stereotypically known as the marriage hub for people in the Latter-day Saint community.

got engaged to him the next, and I was her bridesmaid right after my first year of college ended. The following year I continued to go on dates now and then, all while watching person after person get engaged and continually receiving wedding invitations to put on what was later deemed the "Singles Awareness Fridge." But still no luck.

Then I decided it was mission time.[2] I mean, what better way to draw closer to God and prove to Him I was ready for a tight-knit 24/7 relationship with a companion, right? Besides, I had always wanted to serve a mission. Maybe God had held out on me until then to ensure I would not miss out on this opportunity to serve. So off to the Missionary Training Center I went and from there to the mission field. My mission was an absolutely invaluable experience, but it was not easy.

Sometimes my companion and I got along like two peas in a pod and it was absolutely fantastic! Sometimes, it seemed like we clashed like peanut butter and Sriracha hot sauce (I mean, they're both great, but no-can-do together!). It was filled with joy and hope, excitement and faith mixed in with sadness and disappointment, frustration and self-doubt. Now that I think about it, that's probably a fitting way to describe marriage as well, but who am I to say that?

Post mission, I arrived home a sad, awkward mess—deeply missing the work of the Lord and the people I came to love and not sure how to interact normally with those of the opposite gender anymore, but ready to blaze forward with whatever the Lord had planned for me. And obviously that was marriage, right? I mean, if you connect the dots, that's the logical next big step. At least that's what everyone else was pushing for.

As a young 21-year-old girl, I began to be bombarded with those persistent, awkward questions that have you responding with a fake smile, while inside you're either groaning, rolling your eyes, straight-up crying, or thinking about punching a pillow —"So are you dating someone yet?" "Are there any boys in your life right now (wink, wink)?" "When are you going to get married?" The floodgates were opened, and the pressure was on!

2. At the age of 20, I set aside a year and a half of my life to share the gospel of Jesus Christ as a full-time volunteer missionary for The Church of Jesus Christ of Latter-day Saints in Nashville, TN and Natal, Brazil. While I was a missionary, I did not date and was assigned to serve with another female "companion" that would change every so often.

I tried to put myself out there and make myself "available." I dated one guy for a while, but we both recognized that our paths in life were going in different directions. And so it was back to the single life of ice cream and pizza nights with the girlfriends I loved. I started nursing school, and who has time for boys when your schedule is overflowing with classes, work, homework, tests, sleeping, and eating—the whole mumbo jumbo?

There were a ton of single women in my college, "Nursing students must just intimidate guys because we have a career going for us," I thought. But then I watched the girls in my class get engaged and married one by one. I went on an assortment of awkward first dates—so, boy, do I have good, cringe-worthy stories to tell if you ask me for them—but nothing.

Then one day, it happened. I had pretty much given up on boys by then. It was pointless, I thought. God just has more important things planned for me right now. But one day one of my guy friends brought his friend to my house. I thought Jordan was really cute, but again, I knew it was a lost cause. No hope, no faith, no flirting. Nada. Nothing was going to happen. I didn't even try to impress. Didn't even care about putting on makeup.

All of us soon became friends and we spent a lot of time together. People told me Jordan and I should date, but I would quickly brush them off. We got mistaken as a couple multiple times, but I would just laugh about it and dismiss the notion from my mind. It wasn't going to happen.

Then one day, Jordan shocked me when he asked me out. I was so taken aback, I went into what I called, "Frozen Shock Mode," which is when your perception of reality and what is really going on don't match and you don't know how to respond. But, after recovering, I told him I was in, and the courting began.

My best friend interrogated him, and he apparently did really well. We defined the relationship, and just like that we were a couple. It was like magic! We were so perfect for one another. He was able to listen to me talk about all the gross, nasty stuff I saw in the hospital, appreciate my ability to draw poop emojis, and watch medical dramas with me without getting sick to his stomach. He was willing to pick me up at 6:30 a.m. when I was hit by a semi-truck 30 minutes away from where we lived and pick me up from class to take me to the FrontRunner train station every Friday for my clinical shifts after I lost my car.

He was an amazing communicator, and we could talk for hours about anything. He respected my space and let me have girl time when necessary. He was my first kiss and I was his. We fit together like two peas in a pod! My parents met him and absolutely adored him. "Is this it?" I thought. "Could he be the one?" But despite the fact that we seemed so perfect for each other, for some reason, I felt like something was missing. The thing was, I didn't know what, and no matter how hard I tried to figure it out, I kept coming back empty-handed.

Then, the Christmas before I graduated, I went back home to visit family. Jordan and I continued talking daily and it seemed like despite my doubts about that missing piece, we were doing fine. Then one day we were talking as usual and as our conversation was coming to a close, he suddenly asked if we could talk about something serious. "Go for it!" I told him, not thinking much of it. He then proceeded to tell me that after going to the temple and praying about us multiple times,[3] for some reason he just didn't feel like we were meant to be.

I was kind of shocked. I mean, I had sort of been feeling the same way, but it was hard hearing it from the other person. "I'm so sorry," he said in the most genuine voice I could have imagined. I could tell how hard this was for him. "No. It's ok," I responded. I then told him about my feelings as well, how we seemed so perfect for each other, but it just seemed like for some reason, there was something missing.

The next few months were horrible! I was crushed! Not because he had been mean or even because I had expected everything to turn out differently. It had been mutual. I didn't have anything bad to say about him. But it was difficult all the same. I went to my friends for advice and support. They told me to exercise, watch sad movies, listen to podcasts, let myself feel everything. I tried it all. I had been so close! And yet, it wasn't right. I knew it. He knew it. God knew it.

As I worked to push through the sadness, I was able to see new opportunities open up for me, opportunities I may not have taken advantage of if Jordan and I had still been together, which was comforting in a way. But getting back into the dating game, which now seemed like a literal hunt with predator and prey at times, was a struggle. More

---

3. Members of The Church of Jesus Christ of Latter-day Saints often go to temples to pray about major life decisions and receive revelation from God.

awkward dates. More unmet expectations. More hopelessness. And here I am today, a post-grad Latter-day Saint girl trying her luck at adulting where the Lord has taken me, far away from the Church hub in Utah, still single and sometimes too tired and fed up to mingle.

But through the darkness of doubt, exhaustion, and uncertainty, as this righteous desire seemed to be continuously met with a sturdy brick wall I couldn't and still can't seem to push my way through, God showed up for me. He showed up for me by opening doors going other ways. He showed up for me by giving me opportunities to learn, to grow and enjoy; people to meet, befriend, and love; places to see, explore, and experience.

It was as if He was telling me, "My sweet girl, relax for a second. I have this all under control. Take a breath! Look around! There's so much I have for you! And while marriage is certainly a part of the plan, it's not the only thing in the world that will make you happy. I've got so much more out there for you! That brick wall is not standing between you and eternal happiness with the man of your dreams. You don't have to knock it down with a sledgehammer and race into something that I'm not quite ready for you to meet. I know the way around that wall, and I will take you there. Trust me."

For those of you who have felt or are currently feeling that brick wall up in your face, not giving way or crumbling to the ground as you thought it would, I invite you to remember what Christ really did that week so long ago—the week He descended below all things for you. Yes, you. The week He felt exactly what you were going through, are going through, and will yet go through. The week He experienced the heartache of a young orphaned girl who deeply longs for a family; the week He learned the pains of the sister missionary who is struggling to find people to teach; the week He confronted the anxiety of the young adult woman who can't seem to find her Prince Charming; the week He comprehended the devastation of the young newlywed who is struggling with infertility; the week He knew the exhaustion of a young sleep-deprived mother who gets up every hour of the night as her colicky baby cries; the week He understood the grief of the recently divorced woman who watches her ex-husband get sealed to his new wife in the temple.[4] He knows. He has

---

4. Members of The Church of Jesus Christ of Latter-day Saints get sealed together in marriage for time and all eternity in the temple, though divorce is permitted.

been there. He has descended below it all. He has served and liberated us from our heartache, pain, anxiety, devastation, exhaustion, and grief in the most sacred and love-filled way anyone has ever served or liberated in all history.

So when things don't happen the way we expect, when challenges come that bring us down, we must remember Him and all He has done. We must recognize that, yes, the Lord has many blessings prepared for us that will certainly come to pass if we remain faithful, but maybe it's not time for that yet and there are other things that are more important and need to happen first—lessons that need to be learned, feelings that need to be felt, people that need to be met, and changes that need to occur within us.

Although at times His presence in our life may not be felt in the way we expect, I know that our Savior is always there. If we reach out and cling to Him who rose from the grave on that Easter Sunday two thousand years ago, He will take us in His arms and walk with or even carry us through our challenges and afflictions and make our lives even more beautiful than we could imagine.

Let us not be like those on Palm Sunday who had their faith shaken when the Savior did not do exactly what they wanted when they wanted it. Instead, let us strive to emulate His divine example as He uttered the oft-quoted words, "Nevertheless not my will, but Thine, be done"[5] and continue to rejoice as the people of old did that Sunday so long ago and put our trust in the plan of our All-Knowing and All-Loving Creator and Maker.

5. Luke 22:42

Are you facing any sturdy brick walls in life right now—the big barriers standing between you and a good, righteous dream that you sometimes just want to knock down with a sledgehammer because you can't understand why God would be keeping you from something good that you feel like He would want for you? Are you struggling to understand God's purpose for you or His purpose for this big brick barricade? Girl, tell me about it! Like, for real! Because, it stinks doesn't it?! Am I allowed to say that?

A poster on my wall has a poignant reminder that I read daily, "Trust the timing of your life." Such an important prompt, but one that's so hard to follow. Is it just me? My favorite mug has another short simple phrase that has always given me motivation when that big brick wall just seems to be looming over me in an extra annoying way. In cute, neat letters it states, "Stop Waiting. Start Living." I love that! It helps me recognize that even when that brick wall is standing in front of me, I don't have to put my life on hold until something drops from the heavens to knock it down.

So right now, I have a serious question for you. If God were to tell you that whatever was on the other side of that brick wall would happen in say two, three, four years, how would you live your life today? Think about that. Today I want you to give your dream to God. Tell Him the earnest, righteous desires of your broken heart and ask Him to keep them safe for you and give you strength to trust the timing He has for your life. Then brainstorm with Him about what you can and should do in the meantime, and stop waiting and start living, because you are one strong, independent woman and you have a lot to offer this fallen world. ☺

14

Three Good Things

---

*"[She] who receives all things with thankfulness shall
be made glorious." (Doctrine & Covenants 78:19)[1]*

I don't know about you, but whenever I watch or read the news, I
generally get depressed—terrorist attacks, shootings, natural disasters, sexual assault, divorcing celebrities, dishonest politicians, suicide, murder, and people going to prison for this and that. I mean, sometimes I try to be responsible and stay up-to-date on all that's going on in the world with a hope that, just maybe, something happy and uplifting might be happening. However, I generally come out of my mini up-to-date research session pretty disappointed, running as fast as I can for the first exit sign that I can spot. It's just not the kind of stuff that's going to make my day.

I don't know if there is just a ton of bad stuff going on in the world and the bad outweighs the good every day, or if, for some reason, everyone just seems to care more about all the exciting bad stuff going on. Bad news seems more newsworthy than anything good that is happening in the world, unless good news somehow tops something along the lines of a free buffet dinner in Vegas followed by a spa night with your

---

1. A Latter-day Saint book of modern revelation and scripture.

girlfriends and chocolate lava cake with Italian gelato to end the night—just because. You get the idea.

When I was little, seeing the flag at half-mast grabbed my attention. I generally knew the reason behind it, such as things like the September 11th attack or the death of a well-respected politician. Nowadays, the tragic events that invite our half-mast banner of patriotism seem to be happening a little too often for my liking, and most of them seem to be more aligned with a larger death toll—mass shootings, worldwide pandemics, and natural disasters. This symbol of grief no longer grabs my attention like it used to. My response is more like, "Oh . . . I guess another big depressing thing happened this week. I wonder what it is this time." It's pretty pitiful.

Now, before you start thinking about throwing in the towel on news consumption, I want to clarify that, as depressing as the news is, staying up to date is still important. What I *am* advocating for, on the other hand, is that we make sure that the good stuff we take note of in our lives outweighs the bad.

When I was in college, I took a wellness class for nursing students. I remember one homework assignment I got was called "Three Good Things." For this assignment, my professors asked us to start a gratitude journal and write three specific good things that happened to us each day. They showed us research studies proving that those who did this were happier because they would spend their day looking for the positive rather than focusing on the negative. That seemed desirable enough, so I got to work. Each day I would write down three good things that happened.

At first, it was kind of hard to think of things. But, by day two, I noticed that I was feeling much more grateful for the good things going on in my life and much more excited to find and write down new good things happening every day. There were even a couple days that week that I wrote down four good things instead of three, because I had kept track of all the good things happening and there were more than just three to add to my collection of happy memories.

My journal included entries like, "My best friends and I made quesadillas for dinner and danced around the kitchen while cooking" or "It was a beautiful day today—not too hot, not too cold—a perfect day to be deemed the first day of spring. Riding my bike home from class in the sun made me feel happy. I'm excited that spring is finally here. ☺"

My experience that week made such a big difference in my life that I started sharing it with everyone, including my best friends and multiple girls from church. I met one of my professors in the hall that week and started raving about how much this assignment I was working on was changing my life for the better. It was so amazing and crazy what such a small habit could do! She smiled at my excitement and had me share my experience during the following class.

This simple assignment had such a positive impact in my life that I continued writing down my daily "3 good things" even after my assignment was over. And I still find myself doing it today—over four years later. Because of that, my journals are filled with happy positive memories that brighten my day each time I read them.

Over the past years, there have even been times that I found three good things to write in my journal when, to the outsider, my day may have seemed horrible. The day my car got hit by a semi-truck, for instance, I was able to say that one of my good things that day was that I survived a semi-truck accident with nothing more than some whiplash and bruised knees. I mean, how many people can say that? It was cool seeing how I could transform what seemed like negative things that happened into positive statements of gratitude, which, thinking about it now, is what I believe Christ's Atonement is all about.

Our Savior plays a transformative role in our lives. He has transformed a fallen world into a world of learning and growth. He brings food from famine, life from death, healing from disease, and beauty from ashes. And, by His grace, He allows us to do the same with our own lives. He allows us to transform bad to good, sorrow to joy, contention to peace, and frustration to laughter. Because of Him, we can fill our lives with happy things and good memories that will brighten our days in a world full of downright disheartening news. Because of Him, we can find the courage to say, "The world may be depressing but my life is always good" or "My socks may not match, but my feet are always warm."[2]

So when the news seems a little too depressing and when the half-mast flags seem to line the streets day after day, I can picture the Savior—a "man of sorrows . . . acquainted with grief"[3]—giving me a wink and,

---

2. Maureen McCullough
3. Isaiah 53:3

with a smile on His face, saying, "Hey! I know this fallen world is a mess right now, but remember the trick I showed you. There is still good to be found each and every day." I believe that once we've mastered the heaven-sent gift of finding light in darkness and peace amid the storm, this messy world will seem that much more beautiful, and it can all come down to something as simple as three good things.

How's life right now? What do you see when you turn on the news? Are there a lot of uplifting broadcasts? Or is it mainly things that make you cringe? Have you seen any half-mast flags lately? Does the world seem like a mess? Well, whether or not it does, today I wanted to invite you to take advantage of the God-given gift of gratitude. Find a notebook or dedicate a place on your computer or phone to write down three good things that happen each day. It might not be easy at first, but soon enough things will come more naturally. Then watch your life transform as you focus on the positive and ensure the good in life outweighs the bad.

15

The Blessings of Prayer

Be thou humble in thy weakness, and the Lord thy
God shall lead thee,
Shall lead thee by the hand and give thee answer to
thy prayers.
Be thou humble in thy pleading, and the Lord thy
God shall bless thee,
Shall bless thee with a sweet and calm assurance that
he cares.
("Be Thou Humble,"
Hymn by Grietje Terburg Rowley)

While serving my mission, I had an especially difficult time adjusting when I was transferred from my first visa-waiting mission in Nashville, Tennessee to the mission I had originally been called to in northeastern Brazil. I struggled with the changes in culture, in language, in leadership, and in people, and I experienced homesickness in ways I never had before. One Sunday, during church, I was feeling especially down, so I opened my scriptures and found myself in the Bible Dictionary reading under the topic of "Prayer." I read:

Prayer is the act by which the will of the Father and the will of the child are brought into correspondence with each other. The object of prayer is not to change the will of God but to secure for ourselves and for others blessings that God is already willing to grant but that are made conditional on our asking for them. Blessings require some work or effort on our part before we can obtain them. Prayer is a form of work and is an appointed means for obtaining the highest of all blessings.[1]

The highest of all blessings! Now that's saying something about the power of prayer. These words were somewhat life changing as I turned my attention from my own selfish misery to the mission and blessings the Lord had for me that He could only give me if I was willing to step up to the plate and tell Him to "bring it on!" Once God knew I was all in and I asked Him to throw me a pitch, my life became so much brighter.

I'm not saying the hardships disappeared. My companion and I still darted back and forth across streets from shady spot to shady spot in attempts to hide from the hot Brazilian sun, and we still headed straight for the kitchen every time we arrived at the church so we could open the fridge and freezer to cool off our worn, sweaty bodies. My Portuguese wasn't perfect, and I watched people raise their eyebrows in confusion and look to my companion for an explanation even when I thought I had communicated my message so perfectly (talk about a bullet to the heart!). I still felt regular pangs of disappointment as lesson after lesson fell through and door after door people rejected our invaluable gospel message, wanted to Bible bash with us, or tried to hide from us again and again. Was I really so scary that people would reflexively go into fight or flight mode the second they saw me? I'd say that brought on some blows to my self-image every once in a while!

But, as I continued to pray in those hardships, asking God to help me understand my mission and have the faith and courage to move forward in His plan for me, I began to see the blessings. The beautiful people were so loving as they asked me how I was and kissed my cheek as we walked down the streets even before they knew my name. The Elders[2] were goofy and made me laugh as they became nothing short of brothers to me. I saw miracles as people's once-hard hearts softened and opened up to inviting the Savior and His plan of happiness and salvation

---

1. "Prayer," Bible Dictionary (The Church of Jesus Christ of Latter-day Saints, 2013).
2. Male missionaries

into their lives. I realized that Jesus Himself probably provoked the same fight or flight reaction in the people of His day, and I was able to feel that much more connected to my Savior because of it. We were so in this together!

Since that day, I have continuously asked the Lord in my prayers to reveal what He would have me do to accomplish the mission He has given me. And, let me tell you, the floodgates have been opened, to the point where I'm almost tempted to say, "Okay. Okay. Hold on a second! Slow down a little, please! I'm getting a tad bit overwhelmed here!"

So when the times come when you feel down or depressed, inadequate or unable, or on the days you are bored and just want to binge watch TV shows or scroll through social media, I invite you to get down on your knees and pray. Offer up yourself unto the Lord and ask Him what blessings He has prepared for you and what He would have you do to receive them.

Align your will with His will and secure for yourself and others blessings that God is already willing to grant but that are made conditional on your asking for them. Because let me tell you, He has got some invaluable gifts sitting on His shelf and is just waiting and hoping you will get curious enough to ask what you have to do to get them. Step up to the plate and ask for a pitch so that you can get started on your journey to obtain the highest of all blessings.

How are you doing in life right now? Is everything smooth sailing? Or are there areas of your life that are leaving you feeling overwhelmed? Confused? Inadequate? Hurt? Or scared? Are you experiencing any bullets to the heart or blows to your self-image like I was when I was a missionary trying to thrive in a foreign environment?

First off, if you are, I want you to know that you are so so so so loved! These feelings of inadequacy or pain or the hardships that are scattered throughout your day say absolutely nothing about your worth! Don't let them fool you for a second! I mean it! God loves you so much and He has some pretty awesome gifts on His shelf for you.

So, today, I invite you to get down on your knees and offer yourself up to God. Ask Him about the blessings He has prepared for you and what He wants you to do to receive them. Ask Him to help you align your will with His. Then take some time to listen. Pay attention to the thoughts and ideas that come to your mind. Write them down quick and notice the blessings that come into your life as you take action. Revelation and blessings may not come immediately, but they will come. And who knows? Soon enough you might find out the floodgates have been opened to the point where, like me, you're pretty much almost about to say, "Ok. Ok. Hold on a sec! Slow down a little, please! I'm getting a tad bit overwhelmed here!"

16

Taco Time!

"A friend is a gift you give yourself."
—Robert Louis Stevenson

"Girl! I am taking you to get tacos this week!" Those few simple words I uttered on my first day at church in the Baltimore Young Single Adult Ward[1] changed my life. I had just graduated from college and, after packing up my much-loved, ruby red Ford Escape (whom I fondly named Jackie), I left my college town of Provo, Utah along with the friends, family, restaurants, school, neighborhoods, and mountains I had grown to love and made the 31-hour drive from Provo to Baltimore, where I had gotten my first job as a nurse. My parents flew out to accompany me on the long journey. But after getting me there and helping me begin the unpacking process in my new home, it was soon time for them to leave, and I was left to conquer this new chapter on my own.

It was soon after that that I came to the realization that most, if not all, of us will make at some point in our lives—the realization that for some reason, making friends is so much harder as an adult than it was as a kid, teenager, or even college student. Why that is, I really don't know. Are adults that much more shy and reserved? Or do we just not want to

---

1. "Ward" is another word for "congregation."

put in the extra effort to find people with similar interests now that we are not clumped together in ready-made groups and cohorts by playgroups, classes, teams, roommates, and majors? Whatever the reason, this new difficulty became prevalent in my life, and I was suddenly very motivated to fix it.

In a book about dating I once read (it was given to me by a thoughtful cousin who spotted it at a garage sale after I returned home from my mission), I learned about the power of finding similarities between you and another person and then throwing in hints to do more about it (i.e "Oh! You like bowling, too? We should go bowling sometime!"). So, I decided that could work in friendship-finding just as well, right?

On my first day of church in my new young single adult ward, I was welcomed by quite a few new faces. The male ones generally seemed a bit more excited than the female ones, with the exception of one cute girl with long, braided hair. I remember that her sweet smile and bright demeanor drew me to her in an instant. "Hi! What's your name?!" she asked excitedly as she welcomed me to the ward and city. As I began talking with her, I soon found out that her name was Bookie and that her laugh was contagious.

Now, I'm not sure exactly how this came up, but somehow I found out that despite moving here from Nigeria four years earlier, this girl had never eaten a taco! I mean, what?!?! The second I heard that, I saw an opportunity. It wasn't exactly a similarity, more of a difference, but I recognized that she had a need and I was dying to help her fulfill it. "Girl!" I said unbelievably and excitedly, "I am taking you to get tacos this week!" And just like that, our fate was sealed.

I got a recommendation for a good taco place in the area, and then one evening that week we met up for dinner. I will never forget sitting across from this cute, smiling girl. I could tell we were both a bit nervous and out of our comfort zones but also excited that maybe we had found a new friend. I filmed her as she took her first bite of a taco and made history in her life. Her reaction was adorable. "It's so good! . . . I love it! . . . It's so good!!!" she said between bites. At that point I knew it was a friendship match made in heaven, and so from there my mission began to continue this newly founded friendship.

I invited her over to my apartment to try Chinese dumplings and take a course with me on how to love and make the most of your single life each week. We took the missionaries out to eat pho and sat in her car eating take-out sushi or Wendy's after long days of work. She made me spicy Nigerian spaghetti, which was so delicious I downed two bowls of it for breakfast after one of our sleepovers. We laughed together until our stomachs hurt, and we cried together, though her cry generally looked like her laugh, so there were times when I honestly couldn't tell the difference. And just like that we became tied-at-the-hip best friends. It was the best!

Later on, my bestie ended up moving from Baltimore to Provo (switching places with me). It was sad, but we promised to keep in touch and visit each other. When she left, I gave her a cute fuzzy blanket adorned with tacos. The second she saw it, she burst out crying as the memories of how our friendship began came back.

"Girl! I am taking you to get tacos this week!" That statement I had made ages ago had been so simple, yet at the same time so life changing. And I am so grateful that I was brave enough to step out of my comfort zone and find the courage to say those words, because if it were not for that, I would never have forged an invaluable friendship with a cute, bright, smiling girl from Nigeria.

I once read a phrase that has stuck with me through the years, "Friends are the flowers of life." When I think of flowers, I think of beautiful, sweet-smelling blossoms of all different shapes, sizes, and colors that never fail to brighten my day whenever I see them. Throughout my life, I have made an effort to seek out bright colorful friendships with people of varying cultures, backgrounds, stories, and gifts. I love learning new things from my friends and watching our stories merge as we co-create beautiful memories I will treasure forever.

I have amazing friends who are very strong in their faith and other incredible friends who are very strong in their positivity or resilience. I have remarkable friends who can empathize with me in the workplace and other wonderful friends who can commiserate with me in my academics. I have brilliant friends who inspire and encourage me intellectually, and extraordinary friends who push and support me in my dreams. My friendships are invaluable treasures of support along the unpredictable twisting and turning roads of my life that keep me smiling through it all.

During the Savior's last week of His life, He declared His friendship with us all as He told His disciples, "Greater love hath no man than this, that a man lay down his life for his friends."[2] Christ made friends with so many different people on His journey in life—the majority of whom were starkly different from Himself (i.e. shepherds, wise men, tax collectors, fishermen, lepers, harlots, the blind, and the deaf). These friends supported Him throughout His ministry and helped Him spread the gospel even after His passing.

If Christ Himself sought to build friendships while here in mortality and stands as a true eternal friend to us all, I'd say it's only fitting that we strive to follow His example in pursuing friendships, because "friends are the flowers of life" and I think we could all use some to brighten our mortal journeys any day.

Could you use some invaluable new friendships in life? I mean, who can say no to that one? This week, make an effort to talk to more people. Find similarities with others or needs you can help them fill and then throw in hints or direct invitations to do something about it. You never know where you'll find your next best friend. If you already have a best friend, who's to say you can't have more? I have like four of them and it's wonderful! Because "friends are the flowers of life" and although, one flower is beautiful, in my opinion bouquets of different colors and scents will beat a solo rose or daisy any day.

---

2. John 15:13

17

"Please Mind The Gap!"

---

*"Wherefore, my beloved brethren [and sisters], pray
unto the Father with all the energy of heart, that ye
may be filled with this love, which he hath bestowed
upon all who are true followers of his Son, Jesus
Christ; that ye may become the sons [and daughters]
of God." (Moroni 7:48)[1]*

When I was nine years old, my family moved to Hong Kong from our comfortable, familiar, quaint, well-loved home in Ann Arbor, Michigan. I remember being immersed in a totally new culture with new people, new practices, new norms, new scenes, and new languages—a culture where it was now common to see live fish and sea creatures being sold at the grocery store; where everywhere I looked there were seas of people who looked like my mom—short with black hair and almond eyes; where whenever anyone spoke English it was with a British accent; and where I now went to school with a Thai princess, who came to class every day with a man in a suit who I soon found out was her bodyguard.

As a young 4th grader, who was now considered a "Year 5" student at the International School I attended, my curious young mind soaked all

---

1. Book of Mormon

this newness in like a sponge—sometimes reacting in excitement, sometimes in awe, sometimes in confusion, and sometimes in disgust. I mean I can tell you that I did not want to see the fish I was going to eat for dinner swimming around pitifully before it landed on my plate!

In this fascinating world, I soon became acquainted with the new cultural norms, one of which was the subway—a large, bouncy, long, snake-like, underground transportation machine that stopped at various locations in the new Asian land I now lived in. It was there that I became acquainted with the three different languages spoken by the people here—Cantonese, Mandarin, and British English.

As the subway would roll to a stop, an announcer would come through the intercom, giving quick warnings—first in one language, then another, then another, and although I was fluent in English, it seemed to be a hit or miss as to whether the English that came through those speakers would leave me educated regarding what I should do or leave me confused, trying to comprehend what on earth the announcer was trying to tell us.

One such case of confusion occurred when the subway was rolling to a stop at a new station. Following the Cantonese and Mandarin versions of the announcement, a voice would come through with a heavy British accent loudly proclaiming the weird phrase, "Please mind the gap!" "Please mind the gap?!" I initially thought to myself. "What is that supposed to mean? These people are funny. They don't make any sense! How do I 'mind the gap' anyway?"

Soon enough, however, I learned the translation of this confusing phrase in more familiar American English. Basically, this announcer with a British accent was just trying to tell us to watch our step as we crossed the gap between the subway and the station and make sure we didn't trip. I mean how stereotypically polite, right? Almost twenty years later, I can still hear the simple words of that practical warning echoing in my head, but they have taken on a new meaning for me.

There was once a time where I mistakenly believed that I had to be perfect in order to be loved, that I had to earn my way to heaven. I was raised to be a natural achiever. My entire mission in life was to achieve great things in order to make my family and my Father in Heaven proud of me, and honestly it was going pretty well for a while. I was able to take what I was blessed with, do my best, and achieve things that made me beam as I imagined the smiles on the faces of both my mortal and heavenly parents. I believed I was doing fairly well in life both temporally and spiritually, and it made me absolutely ecstatic.

Then one day, my unrealistically founded beliefs came crashing down when I was hit with a bout of spiritual perfectionism that truly destroyed my mental well-being and what I believed was true happiness. Guilt over the smallest mistakes I had made in life, some from deep in my past, infiltrated my mind and I began to recognize how imperfect I was and how unworthy I was of heaven.

I spoke with people I trusted about it—family, friends, and church leaders, and they all reassured me I was fine, that as long as I learned from those mistakes and moved forward, I would be in good standing with God, that He still loved me no matter what. But for some reason, though it made sense logically, I could not convince my uneasy mind to believe it. I felt like my imperfections had decreased my standing before God, that I needed to be punished somehow—beaten with a few metaphorical whiplashes, or whatever God deemed worthy to regain my standing. It was the absolute worst!

Over time, as I took proactive steps to care for my mental health, the guilt seemed to subside, but I felt like I was never able to regain the same proud, beaming, ecstatic level of happiness I had been living at before, and oh was it disappointing! But I guess I felt I deserved it. I had made some mistakes and so God had to take me down a notch on the happiness scale, and it made sense to me. But man was my achiever mindset frustrated with myself. Then one day, post college graduation, when I was trying my luck at this new thing called "adulting" in the Inner City of Baltimore, MD, everything changed.

In my scripture study that year, I had been trying to differentiate between pride and what I had deemed "humble confidence"—a trait I had noticed so many of the scriptural prophets had embodied in their characters. My question to myself was, "How can I overcome pride and achieve this fascinating, yet super desirable characteristic of 'humble confidence?'"

As I thought about that one morning, the words of the subway announcer in Hong Kong were brought back to my now adult mind—"Please mind the gap!" . . . "Please mind the gap?" That phrase of warning somehow transformed in my brain. It was as if I could hear my Heavenly Father saying:

My sweet girl! You know I love you, right? Mistakes and fears and tears and all? The full package? You don't have to earn that love. You don't have to be perfect right now to join me someday. Get this, kiddo! I sent you a Savior—a brother who loves you more than you could ever imagine, who made up the difference, paid the price, offered to take the beating for all those silly mistakes you've made, so you wouldn't have to. You may feel like you've descended a notch in the happiness scale, but no! That's not what I was doing, my precious daughter! I just needed you to be a bit humbler and ask you to "Please mind the gap," or in other words, be mindful of your inability to achieve perfection in this life.

Yes. There's a gap standing between you and perfection, but whoever said you needed to fill it? Gee! That would be so much pressure! And you don't need that! I don't need you to be a hard-boiled egg that cracks the second it's hit with a fork of guilt. No! I just need you to get rid of pride and take on that characteristic of humble confidence—recognize that you're not perfect but still be confident in my love for you, confident that I've found a way to fill that gap without you having to be perfect. Do you understand, Ash? I love you no matter what! You don't have to be perfect to be loved.

As this moment of clarity washed over me, and this sudden, unexpected message from God started sinking in, I knelt down to respond to my sweet Father in Heaven, to explain what I thought He was saying, to see if I truly understood, to repent of the pressure and pride. And soon enough the tears came as I was filled with a feeling of confirmation and intense love. "Thank You, Dad," I responded. "Thank You for loving me despite my imperfections. Thank You for taking me as I am—mistakes and fears and tears and all—the full package. Thank You for giving me an A for effort when I might deserve a C for some silly, careless mistakes. Thank You for blessing me with humility and confidence in your love. Thank You for teaching me to "please mind the gap."

Have you ever struggled with feeling like you need to be perfect to be loved? With feeling like you just aren't good enough? That you don't deserve good things? That you are doing horribly at "earning your way to heaven"? Today, I want you to take a step back. Recognize that gap between you and perfection in your life, stare it straight in the face, and then get down on your knees and talk to your sweet Father in Heaven about it. Tell Him how you truly feel about where you're at right now. Tell Him your shortcomings, insecurities, anxieties, and fears, about the pressures weighing down on you in life, and then ask Him how He feels about you—mistakes and fears and tears and all. Then watch and listen.

Months before this experience, I had asked God how He felt about me and came out disappointed, having felt I hadn't received an answer. Then on an unexpected morning sitting in my bedroom, He suddenly overwhelmed me with the strongest declaration of love I had ever experienced. So, while I can't promise you that your answer will come right away, I can promise you that it will come and, when it does, it will fill that gap you stared in the face with the most beautiful, pure, invaluable, everlasting love that has ever touched the face of the earth, because you don't have to be perfect to be loved.

18

Spiritual Butterflies

> *"Seeds of faith are always within us. Sometimes it takes a crisis to nourish and encourage their growth."*
> —Susan Taylor

The year 2021 was a weird one for me. I don't know if it was the effects of the COVID quarantine and having too much time alone with myself, but it hit me hard! It was the year I experienced my first big "faith crisis," and that trend just seemed to continue throughout the year with spiritual highs followed by sudden lows where I would begin to question everything I knew to be true. And it was scary. I didn't know what to make of it. I was hit with unanticipated questions about the Church as I struggled to discern between eternal truth and temporary religious culture, and I felt the strong carpet of my faith being ripped out from underneath me on more than one occasion.

I suddenly had the unexpected realization that the Church, at least here in mortality, might not be perfect, and it shook me! I didn't know what to do! I was absolutely panicked and devastated! I felt stuck in this rut of my faith where I felt almost spiritually paralyzed, and I became so scared that I wouldn't be able to escape and that this was going to last forever.

Thankfully, I came out of it alright. But that did not stop it from repeating itself in my life every so often, and those feelings of panic, fear, and anxiety replayed themselves in my mind. During these times I asked questions like, "What is this for? Why would God allow this to happen to me, knowing that I have always been so faithful in the Church? Is the Church really true? Or am I fooling myself? Will I ever get through this? And if so, how?"

As I have experienced these episodes repeatedly, I finally came to a realization that changed my life and found productive steps to take during these dark periods of panic and anxiety that helped me move forward until I saw the light again. My realization was that these periods of spiritual wrestling were actually not crises at all, but instead were gifts from God to help me refine, remold, and re-strengthen my faith in ways I never would have thought to do.

My friends and I were talking about this once, and ultimately, we decided that we did not like the term "faith crises." It sounds so negative and hopeless. Like you need someone to come swoop in and save the day or all is lost. So finally, after much discussion, we came up with a term we liked better. We decided to stop looking at struggles with our faith as crises but instead as transformative periods—periods of time when God invites us into our own personalized chrysalises—something more like "Faith Transformations."

Do you know what a chrysalis is? It's the hard shell in which a caterpillar changes from a larva into a butterfly. To become a butterfly, a caterpillar actually has to digest itself. I know! Crazy, right?! But certain groups of cells survive that process, turning the "caterpillar soup" into eyes, wings, antennae, and other structures until it can break free as a new and transformed being. Over the span of 5 to 21 days, the caterpillar undergoes this strange yet necessary transformation to reach its full potential and become a more beautiful version of itself. As scary as it sounds, ultimately, it leads to something beautiful.

When I think of this process, I can't help but think of how during a faith transformation we enter a so-called "spiritual chrysalis." These chrysalises can feel dark. They can feel lonely. They can feel hopeless. But ultimately, they provide us with the environment we need to foster the growth necessary to reach our true potential, to go on a spiritual journey from an innocent and weak little caterpillar to a majestic butterfly.

As I have experienced various faith transformations throughout my life, I have found specific steps in these trying periods that have helped me hold onto hope and better cope with the anxieties that will inevitably arise. When I begin to sense a faith transformation coming, the first thing I tell myself to do is to take a deep breath and remind myself that I'm ok. This step is for the initial period of panic that hits me. Deep breaths might sound cheesy, but boy do they work wonders for my heart.

Next, I say a prayer and ask God to help me get through this. My goal through these periods of faith transformation is to hold onto pure, uncontaminated truth and what God would have me treasure in my heart while sifting through the messages I receive from external sources. Having God near to guide me through this process, to redirect me when I have gone too far one way or the other, and to encourage me when I am exhausted in my wrestling for truth is ideal, and I would have it no other way. God wants me to succeed. Therefore, I would want no one else as my #1 cheerleader throughout this process.

After connecting and communing with the Lord, I try to "remember my anchor"—the doctrines and spiritual experiences I've had that ground my faith. These will be different for everyone. My anchors each have spiritual experiences to back them up. Some examples are 1) I have a Heavenly Family who love me, hear me, and answer me when I ask questions; 2) I have a Savior who died for my sins, can empathize perfectly with me, and provide me with exactly what I need to do hard things and keep moving forward in the Plan of Happiness; and 3) Priesthood blessings[1] make me feel better, so you will find me asking for one every time I realize I am entering another spiritual chrysalis and need some extra support.

When I have fully recognized, remembered, and embraced my anchor, I then move on to recognizing triggers, pinpointing questions, and being a seeker of truth. I investigate what initiated this faith transformation period. Maybe it's obvious, or maybe it will take a little searching. Was it something someone said or did? Something I heard through the grapevine? Something that happened randomly? Whatever it is, I take a second to recognize it. If it was something that hurt me, I allow myself time to grieve. Then I pinpoint the question that has risen from

---

1. In The Church of Jesus Christ of Latter-day Saints, worthy priesthood holders are able to bestow inspired blessings of comfort or healing from God to those who ask.

these triggers. I ask myself, is answering this question critical to me staying strong in my faith?

I remember, as the amazing Sheri Dew once said, "Questions are not just good, they are vital, because the ensuing spiritual wrestle leads to answers, to knowledge, and to revelation. And it also leads to greater faith."[2] I must let my questions allow me to see myself as a seeker for truth rather than a doubter. That mindset switch makes all the difference.

After careful analysis of my triggers and questions, I find a spiritual mentor—someone I trust and can talk to about my feelings without the fear of judgment or over-validation. I usually try to find someone who has experienced their own faith transformations and successfully worked through the process to grow that much stronger in their spirit and faith.

I remember when I had my first big faith crisis, I immediately reached out to a friend of mine who had made multiple allusions to faith crises he experienced in his own life and yet was still strong in his faith. I quickly texted him: "Hey Dennis. How are you? This is sort of random but I'm kind of in the middle of a sudden faith crisis. They don't happen very often for me . . . I know you have mentioned dealing with faith crises in the past and wonder if you have any words of wisdom for me."

My sweet friend called me in a heartbeat. Bless his big, warm, loving heart! He listened to me tell him about what was going on, he gave me words of counsel when I asked for them, and he comforted me in the anxious, foreign, lonely place I was in. He showed me he loved me and wanted to help by offering to do things he knew I would appreciate. It meant the world!

And while I can't say that I immediately popped out of the faith ditch I was in, he gave me the courage to continue on for a while and keep feeling out the terrain, to recognize how the gospel and Church had blessed our lives and give them another chance.

These faith-shaking crises have happened again and again in my life, each leaving me uncomfortable and panicked, but each time God has provided me with the courage to reach out to those I believe can help, to those who can get down on my level and say, "Hey. Tell me how you're feeling right now!" or "Oh my gosh! I totally understand! I've so been there! How

---

2. Sheri Dew, "Will You Engage in the Wrestle?" Brigham Young University—Idaho devotional, 17 May 2016, www.byui.edu/devotionals/sheri-dew.

can I help you?" Or "These are some resources that have helped me in these situations in the past. I hope they can help you too." It touches me so much to see how God sends these people into my life to find and acknowledge me in my "little lost lamb" stages and help bring me home.

Having a spiritual mentor helps bucketloads in my faith journey as I am able to connect with others who have been through this before and recognize I am not alone. But even then, this journey is very personal, and I might need to give myself time. There is no deadline or due date to figure out where I stand in my faith, so there is no rush processing it all. As uncomfortable as it may be and as much as I want to snap myself out of it at times, the growth that comes from the wrestle will make it so so so worth it.

Finally, I try to remember that this won't last forever, and that God is on my team as I place myself in a truth-seeking role. It's kind of funny because the best thing I can compare the feelings that arise during this time to, at least in myself, is the initial emotions that result from a hard romantic break up that may have caught me off guard. Breakups can be scary, devastating, ugly, and embarrassing and often result in unexpected questions and pain. I get caught in this rut of heartache and don't know how I will ever escape or recover. A strong desire to rush the process of healing sets in and anxiety that this is how life is going to be forever now tickles at my emotions.

But somehow, in some way, often with much self-care and efforts to grieve and heal and love myself, I am able to find a way out of the rut. And, in the process, I learn much about the things I value and want to prioritize and ways to heal and care for myself. I am able to experience all of the positive emotions I once experienced before, maybe even at a higher level, and find a greater appreciation for the highs because I have seen the lows. This was part of God's plan. In order to know the sweet, I have to know the bitter. And becoming more familiar with the bitter can help me appreciate and treasure the sweet beyond what I thought I could before if I let it.

For all of you who feel like caterpillars right now experiencing the uncomfortable growing pains as the process of spiritual metamorphosis seems to be digesting all you have to offer in an effort to transform your faith, your testimony, and your heart, know this: God sees you. He knows where you are. And He sees your great potential and is rooting for you through it all. He wants this process to make you stronger, even though at times you may feel weak. He has every good intention in allowing you to engage in the wrestle for truth.

Latter-day Saint author Thomas McConkie says that faith crises are a part of a natural cycle of spiritual growth, a breaking open to make room for new life and new faith. It is a sign of God's trust in you rather than a sign of abandonment.[3]

In her book *Untamed*, Glennon Doyle says,

> *Pain is not tragic. Pain is magic. Suffering is tragic. Suffering is what happens when we avoid pain and consequently miss our becoming. That is what I can and must avoid: missing my own evolution because I am too afraid to surrender to the process. Having such little faith in myself that I numb or hide or consume my way out of my fiery feelings again and again. So my goal is to stop abandoning myself—and stay. To trust that I'm strong enough to handle the pain that is necessary to the process of becoming. Because what scares me . . . a lot more than pain is living my entire life and missing my becoming. What scares me more than feeling it all is missing it all.*[4]

So rather than resisting the faith transformations that come our way, let us take deep breaths, pray for help, remember our anchors, recognize triggers, pinpoint questions, and be seekers of truth. Let us find spiritual mentors, give ourselves the time we need to process it all, and remember that the discomfort won't last forever and God is on our team. Let us find ways to embrace these periods with courage, knowing that as scary as they may seem, ultimately, these strange yet necessary transformations will help us reach our full potential and become a more beautiful version of ourselves just like caterpillars become beautiful butterflies.

---

3. Thomas W. McConkie, *Navigating Mormon Faith Crisis* (2015).
4. Glennon Doyle, *Untamed* (Random House Publishing Group, 2020), 52.

Where are you on your faith journey right now? Have you taken on the butterfly life and are thriving more than ever? Or do you feel like you're stuck in that deep, dark chrysalis where you and your beliefs are being mixed and digested in the process of spiritual metamorphosis? Are you confident in all you believe? Or are there some topics that make you a bit uneasy when someone brings them up?

Today, wherever you are in your faith journey, I want you to remember that God is with you. Remember that your Heavenly Family loves you so incessantly that there's nothing you could do to distance yourself from that love. They are there for you when you are emerging from your spiritual chrysalises and there for you when you are in the midst of them. Sometimes they take a step back, not because of a lack of love or to punish us for wrongdoings, but to simply let us grow stronger.

For those of you who may be in the midst of a faith transformation, struggling and wrestling as you try to comprehend how God thought this was a good idea, I want you to take a deep breath and remind yourself that you are ok. I want you to say a heartfelt prayer, asking God to be with you and help you through it all. I want you to remember your anchor and hold it like there's no tomorrow. I want you to recognize triggers, pinpoint your questions, and, most importantly, see yourself as a seeker of truth. Then find that spiritual mentor we talked about, give yourself time to work through it and process it all, and remember that this won't last forever, and that God is on your team as you place yourself in a truth-seeking role.

You are amazing! And, as you engage in the wrestle and strive for a better, brighter, and more beautiful becoming, you will see your faith transforming into something more beautiful and glorious than you could ever imagine. You got this!

19

"And They Came with Haste"

I feel like we all have collections of some shape, form, or size. As a child, I went through phases of collecting animal posters and teddy bears, and now that I'm older, I'm more of a postcard or painting collector. I don't know what it is about collections, but somehow having a large and diverse array of something or other seems to spark some sort of pride or joy. And when we take the time to look through these things, it hopefully brings back good memories of times long past.

One of my most special collections to date is nativities—beautiful illustrations or models of the scene of our Savior's birth. This collection idea runs in my family, with my grandma and aunts and uncles all having their own nativity collections, and whenever I travel abroad to a new country, I always keep my eyes open for new nativities to add to both my own and my family's assortment.

I have collected nativities from China, India, Israel, Brazil, Peru, Ecuador, Argentina, and Fiji. I love to see how different cultures interpret the sacred scene and add some of their heritage and tradition to create connection and meaning for themselves. I enjoy seeing the expressions of the various characters: Mary and Joseph and sweet baby Jesus, the wise men and shepherds and even the animals surrounding the scene as they participate in and experience this miraculous event. The story of our Savior's birth is one that has captivated audiences all over the world. It was a life-changing event, even for people today, and so it can hold a dear place in our hearts.

One day, I was studying this sweet story in the scriptures. I had read it many times before, and honestly, I wasn't expecting any big new insights. But as I read Luke 2:16, I became particularly captivated by one specific line I had never really paid much attention to before. The verse described the shepherds' reaction to the angelic declaration of the birth of Christ. "And they came with haste, and found Mary, and Joseph, and the babe lying in a manger."—"And they came with haste."

As I thought about the urgency these shepherds felt after hearing about the birth of their Lord and Redeemer, it made me feel that these individuals were not just random people watching sheep in a meadow nearby. It made me wonder how the Lord had prepared them so that at this particular instant, they felt so motivated to immediately leave all they had and race to see their newborn Savior. They didn't stop to worry about their possessions or procrastinate their journey. They dropped everything they had been doing, left all they had and said, "Let us now go even unto Bethlehem . . . And they came with haste."[1]

These humble shepherds were personally invited by angels to undertake a search for the Lord. However, I imagine that although this may have been the first time they were invited to do this by angels, which definitely took them by surprise, this was not the first time they were invited to do this by the Spirit. It seems that their hearts had been prepared over time for this moment so that when it came, they would feel nothing but joy, excitement, and determination to be a part of this grand event that would go down in history. It made me think, "What can I do to prepare *my* heart for the coming of the Savior, so that when He comes, instead of feeling anxiety, hesitancy, or doubt, I will feel nothing but joy, excitement, and determination to immediately run to meet my Lord and Savior, as the shepherds did?"

---

1. Luke 2:15–16

As I continued to reflect on the story of Christ's birth, I was reminded of the story of the wise men in Matthew 2, who saw the Savior's prophesied star in the east and "rejoiced with exceeding great joy" and immediately left to worship him.[2]

Now, I personally love stars. No. That's an understatement. I adore them! I think part of it probably has to do with the fact that I grew up in Shanghai, China, where it was too polluted to see any stars. I still remember my freshman year of college. I had moved back to the US for school and my roommates thought I was absolutely crazy because whenever I saw the stars, I would freak out and start shrieking in excitement at my ability to see them and how beautiful they were.

I was so grateful that God had blessed me with such an amazing view of the heavens. However, despite the fact that I love the stars, I'm not an astronomer or professional stargazer and can name maybe two constellations? So I'm not quite sure I would notice a new star that popped up in the sky one night. I mean, would you? The fact that these wise men noticed it meant they had studied the prophecies and the heavens and were actively looking up and searching for this sign of the Savior's coming.

In order to be ready for the coming of the Savior, we have to prepare. There's no sitting and waiting around. We have to be up and doing things to prepare our hearts and minds for this special upcoming event. It is so easy to get distracted by the temporal—whether that is school, work, socialization, or (a big one today) technology, among many other things. It is so easy to become preoccupied by our worldly needs and to focus our attention downward at these things, while forgetting the beautiful, miraculous, God-sent blessings that can be so easily acquired from the heavens. But like the wise men, we cannot neglect to look up in our search for the Savior. We cannot neglect to keep our eyes on the skies.

Our Savior has invited each and every one of us to follow Him, but in order to do this, we have to first find Him. In order to search for the Savior, we must first set aside some time for Him in our lives and in our hearts. I know these days it is so easy to make time for friends, for Netflix, for shopping, and for social media. If these things are so easy, why is it so hard to make time for Christ? Why can't we be like the shepherds of old who, when called upon to search for the Savior, immediately

---

2. Matthew 2:10

dropped all of their tasks and possessions and "came with haste"? Why can't we be like the wise men who searched long and hard for that brand new star and who, when they found it, "rejoiced with exceeding great joy" and "[came] to worship him" and bring him gifts and treasures?[3]

Are our hearts and minds ready to be presented as treasures to the Savior? I don't know about you, but I know mine definitely still have a long way to go. But I also know with all my heart that despite our imperfections and our tendencies to look down, our Savior truly loves us, and that He will lead and guide us in our search to come to know Him, as He did the shepherds and wise men, if we but humble ourselves and ask. In doing so, I believe God will bless us in our search for the Savior, so that when He comes again, we too can "come with haste" and rejoice with "exceeding great joy" as the shepherds and wise men of old.

I know from experience how good these invitations can sound on paper, but I also personally know how difficult it is to put aside the temporal and carry through with the spiritual. So today I invite you to start with a prayer. Not just any prayer, but "an earnest and sincere prayer of a humble and pure heart" asking the Lord what you should do today to look up and draw closer to Him.[4] What are some temporal things you should make time to set aside so you can rid yourself of distractions in your search for the Savior? How can you better prepare your heart and mind to present as treasured gifts to the Lord? Write down the answers you receive and then act upon them "with haste."

---

3. Matthew 2:2, 10
4. Thomas S. Monson, "The Search for Jesus," *Ensign,* Dec. 1990.

20

Undefeatable

---

*"As long as we have faith in our own cause
and an unconquerable will to win,
victory will not be denied us."*
—*Winston Churchill*

While serving as a missionary in Brazil, I noticed it was often difficult for people I spoke with to understand how the gospel of Jesus Christ worked with His Atonement. So after much study, thought, and prayer, I came up with a way to help them by incorporating something more understandable into our lessons, and that was the all-time Brazilian passion of soccer, or "futebol" (foo-chee-bowl).

During our lessons, I would ask the people I was teaching to explain to me how a game of futebol worked. They would look at me dumbfounded, but when they realized I was serious, they would begin to describe a soccer game. "Well," they would say, "There are two teams and two goals, and in order to score points, you have to kick a ball into the other team's goal."

I would then respond by asking some clarifying questions. "Alright," I would say, "So, let me get this straight. If you score a goal, are you the only one who gets a point?" They would kind of raise their eyebrows and laugh and say, "No! Your whole team gets the point!"

"Well, what about your team members who are sitting on the sidelines? Do they get a point too?"

"Yeah!" they would respond. "Everyone!"

Then I would ask them to compare their lives to a game of futebol. "Alright. Here's the deal," I would say. "Our life is like a big game of futebol. The only thing is, there are only two teams—the team of our Savior Jesus Christ and the team of the adversary. And, the cool thing is, we actually get to choose which team we want to be on. The weird thing about this game though is we already know who's going to win, because Jesus Christ is the best futebol player in the world, even better than Neymar Jr., because He is literally undefeatable!

"Now, the adversary doesn't require much of his team members. He'll let anyone on his team. But, because Jesus Christ is the captain of the undefeatable team, He requires a few things of anyone who wants to join Him."

"Well, what does He require?" they would ask.

"Well, first, He wants to make sure that you believe in Him. He is the team captain and He needs your faith. Second, He knows we all will make mistakes, so He doesn't require perfection. But He wants us to be willing to apologize when we do make those mistakes and try our hardest not to make them again. Third, He wants us to be baptized and take His name upon us as we try to be more like Him and represent Him as His team members wherever we go. Fourth, He wants us to accept a gift He has for us called the Gift of the Holy Ghost. This gift is special because it will help us know what to do. It will help us understand what plays are good and what plays are bad and warn us when complicated or dangerous situations come our way so we can do all we can to avoid them.

"Then, last but not least, He wants us to be willing to endure to the end—to keep believing in Him, keep apologizing when we make mistakes and keep trying to be better. He asks us to take His name upon us, stay loyal to our team, and keep using that amazing gift He gave us as we continue to play on His side. If we commit to doing these things, He will eagerly welcome us onto the field to play alongside Him. And even when we screw up, mess up a play, or feel like the worst team member, our Captain and Savior, who is our lead scorer no doubt, will never get fed up or turn us away. He will continue to score points for our team, happy to have our effort and support. And, with Him on our side, we are undefeatable."

Now, I must admit, I have personally never been good at sports—gymnastics, soccer, track, basketball, field hockey, volleyball, or competitive swimming. I've tried them all, and I honestly don't think I've ever scored a goal or won a race in a legitimate game or competition that was not practice or just fun and games.

In gymnastics as a child, I could never get far when attempting to climb the rope to the ceiling. At Halloween, my best friend would always climb up and get a piece of candy for me in the bucket that was hanging so high out of my reach. And I know that many have laughed at my clumsiness when they've seen me attempt to throw a Frisbee at Church activities.

Yet, for some funny reason, my lack of talent when it comes to sports has never stopped me from putting in my best effort when I am invited to play an athletic game of any type. It is comforting to know that all that the Savior requires is effort.

Dale G. Renlund once said, "God cares a lot more about who we are and who we are becoming than about who we once were. He cares that we keep on trying."[1] In this lifelong game of futebol, all that the Savior requests is that we keep on trying, keep on playing, keep on running. Although we may be clumsy and make silly mistakes at times, our Savior is understanding, and He is forgiving.

This theme reminds me of one of my favorite poems, "The Race" by D. H. Groberg, which tells the story of a young boy in a large boys' race who is so excited to run and win and make his father proud. Yet, in his excitement, throughout the race, he trips and falls, not once or twice but three times. Each time he falls, he debates whether he should continue to run as each time his chances of winning are decreased. Yet every time he looks up at his father watching him, he can feel his father telling him to "Get up and win the race." And when this tired, sad youngster crosses the finish line in last place, he is welcomed by a cheering crowd all the same, in a way that would make the outsider think he had won. As he goes over to his dad, head bowed low, unproud, he sadly says, "I didn't do so well."

---

1. Dale G. Renlund, "Latter-day Saints Keep on Trying," April 2015 General Conference, churchofjesuschrist.org.

"To me you won," his father says, "You rose each time you fell."

On a large pinboard in my room displaying inspiring pictures and meaningful quotes, on a small colorful piece of scrapbook paper, I have written the last two lines of this poem, "And when depression and despair shout loudly in my face, another voice within me says, 'Get up and win that race!'"

Those simple words remind me that my Heavenly Father is watching over me in the race of life. He knows my strengths, talents, and capabilities. He knows my struggles, weaknesses, and fears. He will never make me run faster than I have strength.[2]

When life gets hard and I look to my Father in Heaven for help, He will give my hand a warm squeeze and say, "Hey, sweet girl! No matter how good or bad you are doing, I'm here. I will show up to every single game of yours. I will be your biggest cheerleader. I will give you refreshing water breaks on the sidelines that will refill your tired spirit and keep you going until you reach the end."

I am grateful for such a supportive, loving Father in Heaven, because effort is all that counts to Him, and no matter if I come first or last and no matter how many times I fall, if I cross the finish line, I have won in His eyes, because with Him, I am somehow undefeatable. How are you doing in the soccer game or race of life? I'm not asking how many goals you've scored or how many miles you've run. I'm not asking how you're doing compared with everyone else. I'm asking if you've chosen a team today, because honestly, it's a day by day, hour by hour, minute by minute decision.

I'm asking if you're confident in the team you've chosen and what you're doing to show your team captain you believe in and want to represent Him. I'm asking if you're feeling energized and running full speed ahead or feeling kind of exhausted and jogging, walking, or even crawling rather than running in the direction you've been told to go. Do you need some water? Or some of those awesome soccer game snacks the moms were always assigned to bring to my recreational soccer games back in the day? Because,

2. Mosiah 4:27, Book of Mormon.

girl, if so, know that you're not the only one. Know that you're not the only one who might feel like they stink at sports sometimes, if not all the time, like me. Know that despite the struggle, you got this. Because effort is all that matters.

You're not competing with anyone; you're not required to make the winning goal; you're not required to run the fastest mile; you're not even required to look super snazzy and like you got it all under control during this whole process. And when you need a breath or some water or some delicious, crunchy Doritos, God will provide. He will never make you run faster than you have strength. He will help you get up each time you fall. He is on your team and with Him, you are undefeatable.

So today, I invite you to have a heart to heart with God and take a little refresher that will fill you up to keep you pushing through and moving forward in this life. Treat yourself to a smoothie or some real delicious crunchy Doritos, take a bath, read a book, get a massage, do a dance—anything that will give you the necessary boost to stay in the game. And when depression and despair shout loudly in your face, picture your sweet Daddy in Heaven cheering you on from the sidelines and saying, "My sweet girl! You've got this! Remember, together we're undefeatable! Get up and win that race!"

21

"Be strong and of a good courage; be not afraid, neither be thou dismayed: for the Lord thy God is with thee whithersoever thou goest." (Joshua 1:9)

One of my favorite music videos of all time is "Brave" by Sara Bareilles.[1] If you haven't watched it before, it's a must-see! All of these people are sent to different, very public places and have to suddenly start dancing all by themselves. They do this in malls, in gyms, in plazas, and in libraries, and at each place the reactions are different.

Some people watch them quizzically or ignore them, others smile and try to hold back laughter at the strange scene, but some actually embrace it and join in. They are captivated by the bravery of these individuals and want to support them in their courageous endeavor. The bravery of that one person gives others the courage to join in, because if one person can do it, they can too.

What are some of the brave moments you have had in life? The moments that required you to pump yourself up a little bit beforehand and completely push yourself out of your comfort zone, the moments

---

1. sara bareilles, "Sara Bareilles - Brave (Official Video)," *YouTube*, 14 May 2013, www.youtube.com/watch?v=QUQsqBqxoR4.

where you faced the fear of failure and embarrassment and rejection head on and plunged into the deep end before you were totally confident in your ability to tread water let alone swim. Maybe you didn't even realize how much courage those moments took because they were the norm or they were expected of you. Everyone else was doing it, so why was it so hard on your part?

For me, my brave moments have included flying across the world to serve as a missionary in a country where no one spoke my language after having taken a Portuguese class for only six weeks. They include running as a candidate for national office in the National Student Nurses' Association (NSNA). They include packing up everything I had and moving across the country to a completely new and unknown city to start my postgrad years of adulting on my own. They include suiting up as a nurse in personal protective equipment to help care for patients with a deadly virus. Looking back on all of those moments, I've realized that more often than not, what gave me the courage to jump in and do these things rather than staying wrapped in a warm fuzzy blanket in my comfort zone was the inspiring example of others.

I knew that other missionaries had been able to get over the culture shock of moving to a new country and learn Portuguese, and that gave me the faith to keep moving forward in the mission God had for me. I had a friend and classmate who had run for and won the national election the previous year for the same position I wanted to run for, and that gave me hope that I could do it as well. My favorite author and mentor had packed up everything she had and moved across the country on her own, and that gave me the confidence to follow what appeared to be God's plan for me and go through with the scary move He had placed in front of me. I had a multitude of colleagues and friends who were suiting up alongside me to battle this deadly virus, and that gave me the courage to walk into the hospital each day with optimism, knowing that I was not alone, and that God had our backs.

The fact that God sent these amazing and inspiring people to help me do the hard and scary and uncomfortable is so comforting! And as I have cannon-balled into the deep end, inspired by the examples of remarkable mentors and friends, it has also been so amazing to watch others follow my own example.

Believe me, I had no intention of setting any awe-inspiring example with my brave endeavors. I was much too focused on following the example of others and of not drowning in the fear and embarrassment that could follow each attempt to do the impossible. But it has been a pleasant surprise side effect that has taught me that bravery is contagious and so worth it due to the blessings and growth that follow.

These fear-striking brave moments have resulted in some of the sweetest and most invaluable memories and blessings in my life. My mission was where I began to experience more love than I had ever felt before both for people and from people—a love that I never even knew was possible. It stood as a testimony to me of God's love for me and for all of His children.

My experience serving as the Chair and Western Representative of the NSNA Nominating and Elections Committee gave me the opportunity to find inspiring mentors and meet and talk with amazing nursing students from all over the country. I bonded in a way I never thought I could with the committee members I served with as we stayed together in hotels and ate yummy meals together every night on our awesome "business trips." It was also the reason I fell in love with wearing suits and with helping those one step behind me find their way through the chaotic journey they had chosen to brave.

My scary move from Provo to Baltimore exposed me to new heartwarming cultures and people and gave me experiences starting my career at an amazing top hospital with so many learning opportunities and wonderful colleagues. And fighting the deadly coronavirus with those same colleagues gave me new perspectives on life and instilled in me a confidence unlike any other that God was by my side and He saw the strength and potential within me to do hard things.

I believe that God's plan for us includes brave moments. It might seem kind of mean of Him at times. During those times of discomfort we might feel a little bit tricked or abandoned by our loving Creator. But God knows all things and He knows that brave moments are valuable and that no matter how scary they are, when we push ourselves out of our comfort zone and go for the deep end, the blessings that follow will be worth any fear of embarrassment or rejection that stand pointing fingers, laughing, and taunting us from the shore. God is the God that walks on water, and He loves us too much to let us sink.

We, like Peter, are here to develop the faith to take that first step out into the sea and then the next and then the next, looking steadfastly towards our Savior through it all. And when the waves get rough and the storm clouds come to tease and torment our fearful hearts, *He will not let us sink*! Let me say that again! Your loving Creator and Maker standing before you in the stormy waves WILL. NOT. LET. YOU. SINK. That is not who He is and that is not what He does. He will always be there to grab your weak and weary hand and pull you up and out of the billowing waves so you can take a breath and find peace amidst the storm.

When sinking Peter cried out, "Lord, save me!", the Savior answered, "Oh thou of little faith, wherefore didst thou doubt?"[2] My personal translation of that statement for myself is, "My sweet daughter, I've got you! Did you really think for a second I didn't?! I've got you! And I will never ever abandon you or let you fall so deep that I can't reach you! I promise. So go out and do those scary things I ask of you! Go out and take on discomfort and fear like there's no tomorrow! Because the blessings I have for you are greater than you could ever imagine and are so worth the fear of any embarrassment or rejection that could follow. It will be so, so, so worth it. I love you and I've got you. There's no room for doubting that. So let's go for it and I'll be

with you to hold your hand and pull you out of the water when you need it. I'll be with you every step of the way."

So let's be brave and do the hard, scary, uncomfortable things that God asks of us that just might push us to our limits. Let's find those inspiring mentors that have gone before us and inspire those that come behind us, and I promise that these brave moments will be so, so, so worth it. We've got this, sister!

---

2. Matthew 14:30–31

Today I want you to look back on all of your brave moments in life. Recognize the people that helped and inspired you to step out of your comfort zone and go for it, and take a second to think about the people you may have inspired by your courageous endeavors. You are so so so amazing for finding the courage to jump in the deep end, and I love you so much for doing it!

Next, I want you to think of something scary you've always wanted to do or you've felt inspired to do recently. For me, my next assignment that sparks the fear of embarrassment and rejection is the pretty simple task of singing a solo at church. It gets my stomach tied up in knots and my heart beating just a little bit faster. But I promise I'm working on it. It just might take a little time on my part. No one said you had to do these things in a split second!

Today, I want you to pray and ask God to help you carry through with the scary task at hand. Ask Him to give you the faith and confidence to jump in and grab your hand when you feel like you're sinking a little deeper than you're comfortable with. I know it makes Him smile when He sees you are putting in the effort to do something courageous, because boy is He courageous and He is one awe-inspiring example of bravery if you can't think of anyone else to mentor you through your journey of faith. You got this, girl! And never forget that God's got you too!

22

Roses in Disguise

"That which we call a rose by any other name would smell as sweet." —William Shakespeare

---

My grandma loved flowers. There is hardly a day I remember going to her house as a child and not being able to find a fresh bouquet of flowers sitting in a vase somewhere. It seems flowers were something always on her grocery list, just like fruits and vegetables and meat and cheese as well as the ingredients to the amazing pies and desserts she would make for us every Sunday evening, when our family would sit at her dining room table that was always decorated with flowers of some sort. She also loved gardening and had a large garden outside her house where, every spring, she would plant flowers of various shapes, sizes, colors, and scents.

Though I'm definitely not as into florae as was my grandma, I was able to appreciate her love for the natural beauty God has blessed us with. For me, flowers are pretty, but my regard for them takes into account the fragrance factor in addition to appearance. Whenever I see beautiful flowers, whether they be in vases, pots, or at the park, the first thing I do is run up and smell them. It is the deciding factor between happiness followed by pursed-lipped disappointment and a double happy discovery to brighten my day.

It's almost as if flowers that smell good have a secret they are waiting to share with the world if we would only stop and pay a little more attention to them. The sweet scent of roses that waft from my aunt's rose bush that blooms every year or the beautiful hydrangeas on Nantucket Island and their strong, sweet smell floating in the sea-blown air—they all hold a dear place in my heart.

Recently, I was reflecting on life and the infamous phrase, "You always want what you can't have." As I've grown older, I've started to see that this phrase can hold fairly true in a funny way. I think the well-accepted example is the fact that when we are kids, all we want to do is grow up. We want to be "big kids." We want to prove our maturity by making our own money, learning to drive, getting our first period (don't ask me why on that one). Our birthdays are the happiest times of the year—a day to truly celebrate the next major milestone and one step closer to adulthood (because adulthood is the dream)!

And then we hit adulthood, and everything changes. We miss the freedom of childhood, the time when we didn't have a care in the world—when we did not have to worry about making money or being responsible for housing, cooking dinner or planning a vacation, paying off student loans or finding a husband. We start dreading our birthdays and seeing them as milestones in becoming that much older and frailer. As children, we also likely weren't so insecure about things like how much we weighed or how many grey hairs and wrinkles we had. Childhood was the life! Can anyone relate to this?

On a personal level, I experienced always wanting what I couldn't have with the many moves I've made throughout my life. Moving to Asia and the UK as a kid proved to be a heartbreaking challenge for me. As a young elementary and middle schooler who loved my home and friends in Michigan, I was not really down for all the adventure that moving to a foreign country might hold. I was horrified whenever I was told that my family would be moving and sort of begrudgingly trudged through life in these new countries for a while. And sure, I had many adventures with my family and friends, but I was so distracted by my self-created misery that I truly didn't get to experience everything to the fullest, and looking back I really wish I had taken the time to enjoy the fun at my fingertips.

Same goes for when I was in college in Utah. I was so set on leaving the second I graduated. Utah was not the place for me! It was too dry, too cold, too hot, too lacking in diversity—the list went on. College was too hard, too stressful, too frustrating, too long, and so on. And then I graduated and moved to the east coast, and all I could think about was how much I missed Utah and how much I missed school—the people, the scenery, the culture, the food, the learning, the challenge, the progress, and the fun. I missed Utah so much that I went back to visit at least three times in the next year. I missed school so much that I applied to grad school within a year of moving. Crazy, right?

So, back to flowers. I think one of the most well-known flowers is the daisy. Daisies are cute and simple—a white wreath of petals surrounding a large yellow center. They are wildflowers that are actually sometimes considered to be invasive species as they colonize lawns and meadows, though they definitely aren't the worst weeds you can get, seeing that they are quite pretty when compared with say dandelions or weeds without flowers.

The other well-known flower I can think of is, of course, the rose. Roses are beautiful. They can be various colors, and they have a splendid aroma that leaves me wanting to bury my head in them and inhale deeply whenever there's a bouquet or large rose in sight. They are definitely flowers that win points in both appearance and fragrance and leave me doubly happy each time I get to interact with them.

For so many of us, myself included, it is hard to live in the present. So much of the time, I think the majority of us are looking to the future thinking that once we reach this goal of graduating or getting this job or making this much money or finding a husband or having a baby or retiring or anything else for that matter, we will be happy and be able to finally enjoy life.

Or sometimes we are looking to the past and thinking about all the wonderful times we had then and comparing then to now. We trudge through life in the disappointment of what we don't seem to have now that we had then, thinking about how happy we were then and how unhappy we are now. I don't know why, but for some reason it is so hard to live in and enjoy the moment, to be mindful of the present, and to be happy today.

After reflecting on this for a while, I came to the conclusion that life is full of daisies—simple flowers that can be cute or pretty at times but can also be considered invasive weeds that we just want to get rid of or get out of. But rather than bringing out the lawn mower or trying to trudge through them, we actually need to stop and smell them because those daisies just might be roses in disguise. They just might have an unexpectedly sweet scent to detect if we only take a second to bend down and take a whiff.

These roses in disguise may come in times of hardship and stress or frustration and difficulty, when faith and hope are key. They may be too easy to miss if we don't take a step back and pay a little closer attention to what we can gain from today, what just might be able to make us smile right now, and what there is to enjoy when we're cranky or grim.

After thinking about this, I asked some of my girlfriends what they considered to be roses in disguise from their pasts. One of my friends who had struggled with an eating disorder for much of her life told me that she had hated going through treatment for her unhealthy habits in a locked down facility and spent most of that time trying to do anything she could to get kicked out. But looking back she wishes she had actually taken advantage of the "roses in disguise" they had offered by participating in groups, making new friends, and benefiting from everything that had been available to her.

Another friend expressed her despair and anger as the youngest child when all of her older siblings moved out to go to college. She did not want to be the only one home stuck with her parents and thought it would be so awful, and she lived her life angry for a while until she realized that being alone with her parents was actually really fun as she was able to develop a unique relationship with them that was different from the relationship any of her older siblings had with them. Her parents became more like siblings and friends in addition to parents. As she enjoyed this time with them, she said it was fun and she didn't mind being a homebody because she got to know the weird, real side of her parents that you only get with close friends. Appreciating this "rose in disguise" phase helped her go from a mad, despairing teenager to a happy, excited daughter and friend to her mom and dad.

Last but not least, a friend told me that when she had her first child, it was really tough dealing with her baby's "bad days," which involved a lot of short naps and crying whenever he was awake. Then one night she was watching a tv show during which a lady experienced a miscarriage. She told me it was really eye opening as she realized how many people wanted babies and couldn't have them and here she was complaining about her baby having a bad day when he was honestly a pretty good baby most of the time. She realized how often she took him for granted when her eyes were opened to how many people wished they could have a child, which helped her appreciate her son and even his bad "rose in disguise" days that much more.

I just want to remind you that, yes, life is filled with wildflowers and weeds, but there are roses in disguise hidden all around us, planted by the Master Gardener and Creator of Beautiful Things Himself. I know it can be so easy to disregard the things going on today and instead dwell in the future or past, but life is short. If we don't take the time to smell the daisies in our lives, we may never appreciate the sweet scent of those roses in disguise hiding in our lives each day.

Let us not pass up the chance to bury our faces in those beautiful fragrant roses in disguise; that we take the time to find and inhale the heavenly aromas of those unexpected sweet blessings from heaven that are sure to brighten our days and leave us extra happy. I know that if we take the time to do this, our lives will be that much more joyful, brilliant, and fun as we welcome and recognize our God's sweet, tender mercies and His hand working to put a smile on our face and a light in our eyes even amidst the wild, weed-filled struggles of the day. Our God loves us more than we can imagine. He delights in delighting us, so let's allow ourselves delight in today and the roses in disguise He has planted in our way.

Take some time today to reflect on the roses in disguise you have either passed up or been able to enjoy throughout your life. Then I want you to say a prayer, asking God to help you be more mindful of the roses in disguise He has placed in your life today and, as you go about your day, make sure you take the time to stop and smell the daisies so you can recognize the roses in disguise. Each time you recognize one, take a second to thank your sweet Father in Heaven for planting that rose on your path and helping you find it. I promise that as you do this, you will experience a newfound gratitude for the present and all the Lord can and is willing to offer up to you that we so often disregard.

23

Settling for Happy Meals

"If ye then, being evil, know how to give good gifts unto your children, how much more shall your Father which is in heaven give good things to them that ask him?" (Matthew 7:11)

My little sister Karin was born when I was seven years old. She was an exciting surprise for me and my five-year-old brother, and although she cried a ton starting out, earning her the nickname "Cry-in," she was the delight of everyone in our family. That cute baby girl quickly turned into a spunky toddler who would passionately sing songs she made up as she strummed the ukulele she got for Christmas one year and ran around excitedly chasing my brother with a water gun in each hand. There are many fun memories I have of the little sister who is now one of my greatest confidants, but one that will forever stick out in my mind has to do with the restaurant that she deemed her favorite during her youth.

I feel like it is not unusual for fast food restaurants to be a kid crowd-pleaser. I mean what kid doesn't want a toy with their lunch or dinner? However, I must say, my little sister's relationship with the Golden Arches was a little over-the-top. Whenever anyone asked where she wanted to go eat, she would excitedly shriek, "McDonalds!!!" Now, that might seem all good and normal for a toddler, but it was when her 3rd birthday came around that we realized the extremity of her obsession with Mickey D's.

One of my family traditions is that every year on your birthday, you get to choose what restaurant we go to for our family dinner. For me as a child, I would pick my favorite buffet or TGI Fridays or, later on, high-end food at the Shangarila hotel in China. If what we ate that special day was undeniably my choice, with no input from any outsiders, I was undoubtedly going to make the most of it—nothing less than the best!

On my sister's 3rd birthday, we gave her the choice of where she would like to eat, and her immediate, unhesitating answer was of course, "McDonalds!!!" My family all looked at each other with dubious yet amused looks on our faces. "Where do you really want to go?" we asked again. "McDonald's!!!" she insisted even more passionately. Again, the amused glances and raised eyebrows. "Well," someone finally said. "It's her birthday—her choice. Let's go." And so rather than going to any fancy or at least stomach-warming restaurant with delicious food that would have been a rare treat, that year for my sister's birthday, we went to McDonald's. And she was off-the-wall excited about her customary Happy Meal.

As my sister has grown older, she has become a complete foodie and I don't think she has eaten at McDonald's in years! With her expanded palate, now food for her is "go big or go home." However, thinking back on that hilarious birthday treat, I can't help but wonder if in some aspects of my life, I am settling for a happy meal when I could have so much more, if in some aspects of my life I lower my standards for subpar, routine, short-lived happiness when I could be appreciating quality, soul-feeding, interminable joy.

I think this is a theme in this world today. Think about all of the "desirable" things the world offers that bring momentary happiness yet are as good for your soul as a McDonald's Happy Meal is for your heart. If you want to go to extremes, you could say things like smoking and drinking and inappropriate intimacy; but if you calm it down a little, you get spending excessive amounts of time on social media, obsessing over your appearance and weight, or binge-watching Netflix shows for hours on end.

When we settle for these things that we think will bring us happiness in the moment without looking at the long-term consequences, what are we giving up? For the first three, it might be healthy lungs, healthy livers, and healthy relationships. For the next three it could be a multitude of things, including, but not limited to, healthy friendships and "family-ships," healthy body images, and healthy self-care techniques. Today it would seem that the adversary is ferociously trying to fill our world with subpar choices that will seemingly provide "happiness." However, at the same time, the Lord is meticulously laboring to help us see through all those lies because He does not want us to settle. He has so much more in store for us than we can imagine.

Have you ever seen that cute cartoon of the Savior reaching His arm out and inviting a little girl to give Him a small teddy bear she is holding? Her understandable response is, "But I love it God," to which He responds, "Trust me," as he holds a larger bear behind His back waiting to trade it for the smaller one. I absolutely love the message this cartoon communicates, because I've seen it played out over and over again throughout my life. What I especially appreciate about that cartoon, though, is the fact that the Savior does not force the girl to give Him the small bear she holds. Instead, it is just a simple invitation, and she is free to choose whether or not to accept.

Just like we let my sister eat at McDonald's that birthday so long ago when she decided that was what she really wanted, our Heavenly Father will ultimately let us decide what we want. However, if we trust Him and choose to accept the invitations He makes, we can take any of those pathetic, subpar adversary-created temptations for short-lived happiness, and He will easily one-up them any day. You want McDonald's? He'll give you a Red Robin's burger with a milkshake to top it off. You want Taco Bell? He'll give you gourmet Mexican street tacos with the meat fresh off the grill and mouth-watering pico de gallo and tortilla chips on the side. You want Panda Express? He'll give you a delectable, lip-smacking plate of P.F. Chang's with a piece of their Great Wall Chocolate Cake. (If you haven't had it, believe me. It's to die for!)

Our Savior knows the way to true happiness, and if we trust Him, we will never have to settle for second best, third best, or worst best because He loves us infinitely and doesn't want us to be content with anything less than all He has for us. If we want, we can settle for Happy Meals, but then we just might miss out on the joyous feast of a lifetime He has in store for us if we but accept His invitation and trust Him.

What are some ways you have been settling for Happy Meals recently? Is there anything you know isn't great for you in the long run that God could one-up if you trust Him and are willing to make the sacrifice? Take some time to reflect on that today and then talk with Him about what areas of your life you could make more joyous, more soul-feeding, and more beautiful in the long-run by giving up the subpar happiness you've been settling for. Together with Him, create a plan to hand Him the small teddy bear you love in return for the best surprise of a lifetime.

24

The Gift of Pain

"Behold, happy is the man whom God correcteth: there-
fore despise not thou the chastening of the Almighty:
For he maketh sore, and bindeth up: he woundeth, and
his hands make whole." (Job 5:17–18)

I recently fell in love with the book of Job. I had never really studied it before until one day I was invited to lead a gospel discussion on the topic of patience. And when I think of patience in the scriptures, I naturally think of Job. "Don't ever pray for the patience of Job!" someone once warned me when I was serving as a missionary in Brazil.

At the time, I semi-knew the story. Something about a good man who was faced with trial after trial after trial after trial and through it all somehow seemed to continue in his faith, praising God day and night? But the day I actually sat down to skim through it in preparation for this gospel discussion, I was surprised.

Yes, Job was a righteous man who had been blessed with great riches, and yes, he did face trial after trial after trial after trial. But his reactions to his trials were honestly not as perfect as I had previously thought. In fact, they were quite natural—feelings of confusion, self-blame, depression, and unworthiness; questioning the purpose of his trials and his own purpose on earth; seeking God and pleading for relief; and getting support from friends (although can I just say, reading how Job's friends tried to be there for him is pretty humorously sad, because they were kind of like the worst friends ever at making him feel better! One of them even called him a "worm" at one point. Like, "what?!?!"").

But the true takeaway from this famous story is that through his bulk load of trials, this humbled man was able to learn that pain is not always a punishment and, in fact, it can be a life-changing gift that will bring increased knowledge, understanding, and growth and transform the heart and soul into precious gold.

Nobody likes pain. I'm pretty sure that's a fact. I mean whoever said, "I would love to feel some heartache, shame, embarrassment, sorrow, and physical pain on a 10/10 scale?" or "I think today would be a great day to be bullied or put down or receive a metaphorical slap in the face?" Yeah, no! Doesn't happen! And yet there seems to be a daily mass production of these painful emotions and all of these pain-invoking acts throughout the world.

I know the world isn't perfect, but if pain were really that horrible of a thing, I don't think God would have let it slip through the keyhole to our universe. No way! He's more powerful than that. But, for some reason, He did. Job's story implies that God allowed Satan to try Job. The question is, what is that reason?

The book of Job recounts the story of Job's once nearly perfect life that is transformed in an instant. He loses everything!—his family, his possessions, and his property. Then, as the cherry on top, he is plagued with boils—painful, pus-filled bumps that form under your skin when bacteria start tangoing with your hair follicles. (Yeah. They're not the most graceful, in-tune dance partners, but they don't seem to care. I guess they just want to have some fun.)

It's so fascinating watching Job's story of pain turn into a journey of faith as he starts off absolutely distraught, questioning why he was ever born and what horrible thing he had done to deserve such a horrendous punishment. Soon though, he progresses to a mixture of distress and pleading to God for relief, trying to reason with God about his afflictions. As he connects with God, his testimony and trust in Him begin to grow as he confidently testifies, "Though he slay me, yet will I trust in him . . . [and] He also shall be my salvation . . . For I know that my redeemer liveth."[1]

Did you know that the well-known hymn "I Know That My Redeemer Lives"[2] is actually quoting Job in the midst of his heartbreaking and painful struggles? Like, jaw drop moment, right?! Job recognized that although he was suffering beyond anything he could have ever imagined, his pain would be redeemed and that's what mattered.

He goes on to state, "Will [God] plead against me with his great power? No; but he would put strength in me. . . . He knoweth the way that I take: when he hath tried me, I shall come forth as gold."[3] Wow, right?! Yeah. Read it again if you want! Just, wow!

You know how gold is purified through a refiner's fire? How metal can be made into beautiful instruments only through a refining process that requires burning and beating, stretching and bending in its process of becoming? Well, it seems that we require some of what appears to be painful refinement in our process of becoming as well.

Quentin L. Cook said, "The refiner's fire is real, and qualities of character and righteousness that are forged in the furnace of affliction perfect and purify us and prepare us to meet God."[4] Our Heavenly Father loves us so much and cares so much about our growth and becoming that He gave His Only Begotten Son so we could experience the pain that would transform us into beings with the capacity for eternal happiness, joy, and straight-up bliss that He has. To Him, it was worth it. And He knows us perfectly, so I'm thinking it will be worth it to us too.

After making this realization, I've consciously changed the way I look at heartache and hardship. After becoming familiar with Job and his story, I've tried to see pain as a gift. Every time something upsetting or embarrassing or heartbreaking or frustrating occurs in my life, I try to catch myself, take a deep breath, and concentrate for a second. "Where is the gift?" I ask myself. "There is pain, so there must be a gift. What is my gift of pain in this?" And as I focus, each and every single time, I find the gift my Father in Heaven has prepared for me in the refining fire. It

---

1. Job 13:15–16; 19:25
2. "I Know That My Redeemer Lives," *Hymns,* no. 136.
3. Job 23:6, 10
4. Quentin L. Cook, "The Songs They Could Not Sing," October 2011 General Conference, churchofjesuschrist.org.

could be a lesson to take with me into the future. Other times it's a passion about a certain cause or subject. Sometimes it's even a nudge to seek support or practice a little more self-care. But no matter what the painful experience entails, the gift is always there. There is always a gift in pain.

When it comes to gifts of pain, I have found that taking the time each night to reflect on my day and write down what I call "Learning Moments" has helped me tremendously. These "Learning Moments" are painful experiences or mistakes either I myself or others have made that day that I have chosen to learn from. Some examples of my learning moments include:

- When you exit the Philly temple parking lot, you will be turning onto a one-way street, so you probably want to ensure you are turning the right way before making the turn to save yourself from honking, embarrassment, and complications.
- Make sure you turn the bed alarms on for all of your patients that are at a high risk for falling at the hospital or one of them might decide to get out of bed and face the scary consequences on their own.

As I have started this habit, I have found that I am not only able to stay true to the promise I made to the Savior to apologize and repent when I make mistakes, but I am also able to be that much more merciful to myself as I recognize that I am a learning, growing work in progress, and that pain isn't actually always self-inflicted.

Russell M. Nelson once said, "We all need to remember: men are that they might have joy—not guilt trips!"[5] And I wholeheartedly believe this to be true. "Our task is to become our best selves, [because] one of God's greatest gifts to us is the joy of trying again, for no failure ever need be final."[6]

In her best-selling book *Untamed*, Glennon Doyle talks about how we can use pain to become:

I am here to keep becoming truer, more beautiful versions of myself again and again forever. To be alive is to be in a perpetual state of revolution. Whether I like it or not, pain is the fuel of revolution. Everything I need to become the woman I'm meant to be next is

---

5. Russell M. Nelson, "Perfection Pending," October 1995 General Conference, churchofjesuschrist.org.
6. Thomas S. Monson, "The Will Within," April 1987 General Conference, churchofjesuschrist.org.

inside my feelings of now. Life is alchemy, and emotions are the fire that turns me to gold.[7]

I love this so much! The gift of pain is precious and when God has tried you, I stand by Job in saying you "shall come forth as gold."

My invitation to you today is simple—find your gift of pain. Recognize the pain in your life right now. It could be anything that invokes guilt, shame, embarrassment, fear, doubt, or frustration. Then dig deep and find the gift in the pain. Recognize the learning moment God has for you in the hardship you are experiencing, thank Him for the power He has given you to do hard things, and use it to become the woman He would have you be.

---

7. Glennon Doyle, *Untamed* (Random House Publishing Group, 2020), 51.

25

Enough

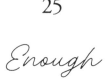

"Our sufficiency is of God." (2 Corinthians 3:5)

Throughout my life I have constantly felt a need to prove myself—to show people that I'm good enough, smart enough, strong enough, and pretty enough—to earn acceptance, approval, applause, and acclaim. Social media has taken that to the extreme! "How many likes and validating comments did I get?! How many people watched my Instagram story all the way to the end?!" I pretend not to care, but that doesn't stop me from checking Facebook constantly the day I post something to see where I stand in terms of acknowledgement and recognition. My brain craves the validation that I am doing amazing, that I am worthy, and that I am enough. It's honestly exhausting. Is it just me, or have you ever felt that way?

The pressures of the world bang down on us like a 100lb weight we're trying to lift while balancing on a tightrope all while attempting to keep a calm expression plastered on our faces so no one in the audience can see we're struggling because we have to at least look like we have it together. The world shows us pictures of skinny models in bikinis while we are already self-conscious enough in a one-piece. A ward member got into school at the university of your dreams while you were just put on the waiting list. A friend got your dream job while you are consistently coming up empty-handed in your job search. A classmate seems to talk constantly about her daily workouts while we might prefer eating to exercise. Our colleague posts about all the delicious-looking gourmet food she meal-preps for the week. As a newbie in the kitchen you ask for some recipes, to which she responds she doesn't use recipes; she doesn't need them. It's a wonder we don't collapse under the pressures of our worldly foes of vanity and comparison.

Earlier this year, I came across a definition of the word "vanity" that really stuck with me. According to the definition I found, vanity is the act of placing the opinions and approval of others over the opinion and approval of God. I think a prime example of this is the wicked queen from Snow White who spends half her time standing in front of a magic mirror asking, "Mirror, Mirror, on the wall, who's the fairest of them all?" with the hope and expectation that the mirror will say, "Well, you of course! You're obviously the most amazing and fair and beautiful and smart person on the planet!"

How much time do we spend a day seeking the opinions and approval of others in the world? How about time spent seeking the opinion and approval of God? I think it's safe to say that I'm definitely falling short in the second category. I may not have realized it initially, but I can see now that I have definitely fished for the validation and approval of others and been crushed when I was denied, whether that was on social media or in person. So how do we change this up?

One day, I was listening to *The Girls Night Podcast* with Stephanie May Wilson, about something very similar to this topic, and while I was listening, the guest speaker said, "We have to act from significance, not for significance."[1] As I reflected on that and the opinion and approval of God I had been so lax about, I had a light bulb moment! (Aren't those just the greatest?!) In that moment it was as if God was saying, "My sweet girl! You are already significant, worthy, and enough to me. There's nothing you can do to make yourself more or less worthy of my love."

Reflecting on that a bit more, I realized that it was true. God loved us before we were even born. Before we even did anything to make Him love us, we were significant to Him; we were worth it to Him; and we

---

1. Stephanie May Wilson, "Girls Night #101: How to Navigate Big Life Transitions with Faith," *The Girls Night Podcast*, 10 Aug, 2020, https://www.girlsnightpodcast.com/library/101.

were enough to Him. We meant so much to Him that He took one look at the Fallen World He foresaw and thought, "Okay. This is a problem! Now my sweet kiddos won't be able to come back home to me! I don't want to lose Emily or Maria or Zahra or _____ (insert your name here) or Matthew or Dakota or Juan or Li. It would break my heart and pierce my soul to the very core. There must be some way to solve this problem! There must be some way to get them back to me!"

And when He found out the way, it must have pierced Him to His very center to know that in order to get Katie and Gabriela and Crystal and _____ (insert your name here) and Ethan and Matheus and Dmitriv back, He would have to give up something He loved so much! He would have to give up His baby boy! His Perfect Son! His most obedient follower!

Just take a second to imagine that. Imagine having to give up one of your babies in order to save all of your other kids. And not only that, imagine having to watch your baby boy be tortured and spit on, whipped and tormented, accused and crucified. It's such a horrible nightmare! The pain must have been inconceivable even thinking about it! And yet, He thought you were enough.

You were enough for Him to go through that unimaginable pain. You were enough for your Brother Jesus to agree to the plan and say, "Yeah. I'll do this for you, because you're my sister and I don't want to live without you. Life will not be the same without you. Life will not be complete without you. I love you. We are family, and I don't want to lose you. I want our family to be forever."

You were enough for the All-Knowing, Almighty Creator of the stock market to take one look at you and say, "She's worth it! I want to invest in that girl right there, because I know she has amazing potential and although she might not feel like she's all that great, I know she's enough and I love her more than I can even say, no matter what she says or does or feels. I love her!"

Whoa! Isn't that crazy to think about?! Isn't it crazy to know that nothing we do on earth will increase or decrease our worth to God—that we are already worth it and enough to Him and that nothing can change that? Let that soak in for a second.

I don't think it's fair to the worthy spirit inside of us that is considered enough before God when we spend our lives comparing ourselves to others and constantly feeling like we are falling short. I don't think it's fair that we let others be our judge when we have a Perfect "Supreme Court" Judge who has already deemed us worthy of His validating love no matter where we are in life and no matter where we stand in comparison to others.

How does comparing ourselves to others serve us? Who decided comparison would be a good friend? How has comparison helped you—the one who was already deemed enough by your Almighty Creator and Maker—throughout your life?

The truth is that it doesn't matter that some people are skinny bikini models or that your friend is going to your dream university. It doesn't matter that someone has a job that you would love or that your classmate does daily workouts and your colleague has a knack for cooking. IT. DOESN'T. MATTER! Because the gifts or talents or skills or aspirations they have don't minimize your worth, don't steal your value, and don't make you subpar. Your worth is constant in the eyes of your Family in Heaven and it has been at that same great level of love since before Day 1.

Nothing you do or say will ever change that level of love. It is there for you and will always be there for you to rest your tired, exhausted, and pressure-filled spirit on whenever vanity or comparison start knocking on your door incessantly tempting you to invite them in because they brought chocolate or pizza or burgers or milkshakes and praise and love and acceptance and glory. (Don't let them tempt you! Because they will try!)

So, even though at times you may feel inadequate, undeserving, imposter-like, or even worthless, I want to send you a little message from your Family in Heaven today, and it goes something like this:

_____ *(insert name here),*

It's been a bit since we last saw you in spirit, and my how you have grown! We can remember the day you were formed and created. You were created perfectly and beautifully. There was no flaw in your appearance, in your potential, in your gifts, and in your dreams. We sent you out into the world with full faith that you would recognize the strength you have to overcome any trial or challenge, to stay true to what is right and good, and to thrive on this mortal adventure we invited you to partner with us to create.

You knew it wouldn't be easy but you decided you were going to go for it. We were so proud of you! We loved you from the beginning and we still love you today. You meant the world to us as we worked to figure out how to overcome the fallen nature of the earth and were faced with the biggest sacrifice of all time. But you were enough—enough to make the sacrifice worth it, enough for your Brother to willingly step up to the task, and enough to make the pain seem but a moment in the eternities.

We could not bear the thought of losing you. We knew that you were worth it. And so Jesus went down and paid the ultimate price for the ultimate prize—and that precious prize was you. _____ (insert your name here), we know that life isn't easy. We know that there will be many disappointments, many difficulties, and many disheartening moments. But don't let those ever make you doubt your worth, doubt your importance, or doubt your significance to us, because no matter what you do, you are enough in our eyes. We love you and are with you in Spirit!

Much Love,

Your Family in Heaven

---

*Today I want to invite you to take some time to evaluate where you stand in the world of vanity and comparison. Have you let these maleficent creatures into your house when they started tapping on the window? Or are you doing good at holding them off? Are you putting the opinions and approval of the world over the opinion and approval of God? Or are you trusting your pre-determined worth in the eyes of your Family in Heaven? And on the days when you are struggling, when you can't seem to feel good enough, worthy enough, significant enough, important enough, read the little postcard from your Family in Heaven again and take the time to recognize that it doesn't matter what the world says. Try to start acting **from** significance instead of **for** significance because you have already been deemed enough and are worth it to the Creator and Maker of the Universe.*

26

Second Chances in the Sacrament

"Yea, verily I say unto you, if ye will come unto me
ye shall have eternal life. Behold, mine arm of mercy
is extended towards you, and whosoever will come,
[them] will I receive; and blessed are those who come
unto me." (3 Nephi 9:14)[1]

When I was baptized as a little girl, I promised myself and God that I would never, ever, *ever* sin again. Yes, I know. That seems absolutely ridiculous, but it happened all the same. And sure, that held true for what—a few hours maybe, a day max, until my little brother said something that made me mad and I lost it, or something along those lines? And then, guess what? I broke my promise. And I was devastated! So I did something along the lines of tell my brother I was so, so, so, so sorry and tell God I was so, so, so, so, so sorry, and then I made that same promise again and I tried it again. But before I knew it, I had made another mistake. So, I made that vow again, saying, "God, this time for real! I will never be bad again!" For some reason I thought

---

1. Book of Mormon

I was different from everyone else in that I could be perfect, and it just wasn't working out.

I made more and more mistakes and each time I did, I got more and more frustrated and tired and devastated and just thought, "Boy! This is so stupid! If only I could be baptized again and be made clean again and get another true chance to be perfect again." Every time I saw someone get baptized, I was downright jealous of them and the chance they had to be made clean again. Now, that may sound silly, but that was a true thought and it all came because I had never been told exactly what the sacrament was, exactly what the sacrament meant, exactly what the sacrament stood for.

To me, as a young child, the sacrament just seemed like a mini snack we were supposed to eat each week while thinking about Jesus and, in part, that was true. But it is really so much more than that. What I didn't understand was what that small bite of bread and tiny cup of water truly represented. It represented renewal. It represented a second, 30th, 400th, 5,000th, 60,000th, 700,000th, infinity-eth chance.

If I had known that, I think it would have given me hope at such a dull moment when I realized perfection was out of my reach here in mortality. It would have given me faith that despite my shortcomings, God still loved me enough to say, "Hey. I know you came up short this week, my little girl, but you tried your best. You were genuinely sorry for the mistakes you made, so I forgive you. Let's try again, shall we? See if we can do any better this time? And, if not, we'll try again, and again, and again, and again. I know life is hard, but you got this! I'm here for you. We'll do this together, and someday, it will all work out as long as you don't give up, as long as you keep putting in your two cents, as long as you keep trying."

What I really didn't realize back then was that, in all actuality, the chance to renew your baptismal covenants by partaking of the sacrament each Sunday is pretty much a chance to unofficially be baptized again, to recommit to remembering and following the Savior, and to recommit to trying to be perfect again despite our flaws. It's a chance to lay our sins on the table and say, "I am so sorry! I promise, I'm going to try my best to never do these things again!" And it's a chance to be made clean again as the Lord sees our genuine, broken hearts and contrite spirits striving to be better. As we seek to understand, prepare for, and take advantage of this sacred, symbolic ritual we have the opportunity to participate in every week, we are armed with a truly powerful piece of artillery for our eternal growth and progression.

Honestly, I didn't truly understand the importance of the sacrament until I reached my adult years when I began working as a nurse in Baltimore and was one day faced with the fact that I was going to miss church for three weeks in a row due to work and travel. During those three weeks, I was suddenly very aware of the privilege I was missing out on—partaking of the sacrament each week. I could feel something missing inside of me and was suddenly filled with an intense longing to be reunited with the opportunity to show my Savior that I still loved Him, that I still believed in Him, and that I was still trying to be better.

I wanted to show Him that I still wanted to stay true to that promise I had made so long ago as an eight-year-old girl the day I decided to take His name upon me and receive the amazing and precious gift He had for me—the Holy Ghost. I wanted Him to know that I hadn't given up, that I was still on His team, and that I would never leave.

Now, I do not recommend skipping church for a few weeks to fully appreciate the sacrament, but I do recommend taking the time to remember what the sacrament really means as you partake of it each week. It is a symbol of your faith and repentance, a symbol of that promise you have made with God, a symbol of the gift He has given you, and a symbol of your perseverance and endurance to the end. It is you telling your Heavenly Father that you still love Him and want to be on His side and that, no matter how bad you are at the sport of life, you're going to keep on trying to the best of your ability to score points for His team.

And it is your Father in Heaven telling you with a smile, "I'm so proud of you for all you've done, little one. Yes, you may have made some silly mistakes this week, but guess what? Practice makes perfect." And with a wink, He sends you off into the upcoming week to practice perfection once more for the second, 30th, 400th, 5,000th, 60,000th, 700,000th, infinity-eth time. Truthfully, the numbers don't matter. I mean, who counts how many times they've taken the sacrament, right? All that really matters is that you showed up to take the emblems He offered you, to renew, recommit, and refuel yourself to take on the life He's given you with Him by your side.

This week when you take the sacrament, I want you to reflect on what it really means. Each Sunday is pretty much a day to unofficially be baptized again. Are we treating it like that in our excitement and preparation? Are we truly appreciating the chance we've been given to lay our sins on the table once again and say, "I am so so so so sorry! I promise, I'm going to try my best to never do these things again!" and be made clean again as the Lord sees our genuine, broken hearts and contrite spirits striving to be better? Are we paying attention to the chance we have to show our Savior we still love Him, that we still believe in Him, that we are still trying to be better, and that we still want to stay true to that promise we made so long ago on the day we were baptized? For me, I learned that the sacrament was my way of showing my Savior that I hadn't given up, that I was still on His team, and that I had no intention of leaving. Take some time to ponder and reflect this week on what this sacred symbol means to you.

27

The Best Surprise

"Remember the worth of souls is great in the sight of God . . . And if it so be that you should labor all your days in crying repentance unto this people, and bring, save it be one soul unto me, how great shall be your joy with him [or her] in the kingdom of my Father!" (Doctrine & Covenants 18:10, 15)[1]

There was one day on my mission in northeastern Brazil that my companion and I were eating lunch at a member's house. Afterward we asked the member, whose name was Claudio, for suggestions about who we could teach. He sadly told us he didn't have any. As my companion and I got ready to leave, Claudio walked over to his daughter's 14-year-old friend who was over. He asked her what her name was and if she liked "surprises." When the girl, whose name was Rwanda, said yes, Claudio excitedly said, "Rwanda! I have an awesome surprise for you! Can I go over to your house one day this week to bring it to you?" She said it was okay and gave him her address. Claudio then asked with a smile on his face, "Do you like chocolate?" When she said yes, he replied

---

1. A Latter-day Saint book of modern revelation and scripture.

grinning from ear to ear, "You are going to love this surprise!" As we were leaving, he slipped Rwanda's address into my bag.

Afterwards, I thought, "Well, that was pretty awesome what Claudio did, but what's Rwanda going to think when we show up at her door as the 'awesome surprise' he promised? Well, we went to her house and, while we didn't bring chocolate, to make the story short, by the second lesson, Rwanda had gained a testimony and wanted to be baptized. From this experience, I learned two very important things. The first is that you never know who is prepared to accept the gospel. The second is that the gospel of Jesus Christ is the best surprise you can give anyone, even better than chocolate, and we should never be too scared to enthusiastically give it to others.

I absolutely adore missionary work! I know it can seem awkward at times as you try to bring up sensitive religious topics that you're afraid will make people feel uncomfortable, but it really doesn't have to be all that awkward. When I moved out to Baltimore, I was surprised by how curious everyone was about my religious beliefs. I am always very open about the fact that I am a member of The Church of Jesus Christ of Latter-day Saints on social media. In my day-to-day discussions with people I also don't hesitate to talk about how I went to church or an activity with members of my church congregation that week. This often sparks further questions, and the news that I am a Latter-day Saint or a Christian always seems to spread fast among the people in my community.

When I first arrived in Baltimore, my new Jewish roommate, Katie, would regularly ask questions about the Church as she saw me constantly leaving the house for church and various church-related activities. I took the missionaries out to eat lunch every week and she would give me restaurant recommendations and always ask how it went afterwards.

One day, Katie surprised me by asking if she could join me and the Elders[2] for lunch. Uh . . . of course, I said yes! It was heartwarming to watch her quickly bond with the Elders and, soon enough, she became a regular attendee of our weekly lunches. She grew to love the missionaries and, when one pair left, she was always excited to meet the next and would keep in touch with those who left. She came with me to a Family

---

2. Male missionaries

Home Evening[3] and a regional Church activity and even took the first two discussions as she was curious to learn more about our beliefs. She wasn't interested in being baptized, but it was so cool seeing her genuine desire to know who I was as a member of the Church and what the Church meant to me.

After I left, Katie got a new roommate and had some pretty horrible experiences with her. One day, while she was venting to me over the phone about all that was going on, she paused and said, "Ashley! I don't think I am ever going to be able to have another roommate again unless they're Mormon!" I thought that was pretty cute. It was comforting to know that, because of me, my roommate now saw the Church and its members in a good light.

One magic trick I've come up with for sharing the gospel is so simple it might sound dumb, but I assure you it works! Throughout my life there have been days that I have knelt in prayer in the morning and asked God to bless me with a missionary opportunity that day, and God does not hesitate to deliver on that one!

There was one day that I prayed this specific prayer before leaving for work. I was assigned to care for a particularly needy patient at the hospital that day who was difficult to please. She was depressed and very tearful at times. As I continued to care for her, I picked up hints that she was a Christian by the things she said and the things she had in her room. Towards the end of the day, as I was comforting my tearful patient, I felt prompted to bear my testimony to her that God knew her by name and that He was with her during this difficult time and would not require her to run faster than she had strength. It was so gratifying to see her face light up and her countenance change from one of despair and downheartedness to one of hope and faith.

On another occasion, I said a morning prayer asking God to help me love my difficult patient better that day. She was also Christian, and that morning I found myself in a deep discussion with her as she was sitting on the toilet in the bathroom. (Lemme just clear this up! That is actually quite normal in the hospital when people are high fall risks and you can't

---

3. Family Home Evening is a weekly event in The Church of Jesus Christ of Latter-day Saints in which family or friends get together to participate in uplifting activities and spiritual discussions.

leave them alone in the bathroom. In fact, conversation kind of makes things a little less awkward sometimes.)

Soon, I was bearing my testimony to her of the love of God and the commandment to "love thy neighbor as thyself."[4] We talked about how she may have spent her life loving her neighbors a bit more than she loved herself and that now was a time for self-care and self-love as she struggled with illness and affliction.

I later asked my patient if she would like to speak with one of our chaplains. (Can I just say, hospital chaplains are absolutely awesome?! They're pretty much like on-call therapists with a deep connection with God! They provide so much support for our patients who speak with them.) Her response was, "No. I think I'm good. You were my chaplain today." I was a little taken aback by her genuine compliment, but it really touched my heart to know that God had sent me to help my patient meet her spiritual needs that day.

I had another experience at work one day that happened after I said a prayer for missionary opportunities. This one actually happened with my colleague. At one point during the day, one of my colleagues came up to me and asked me if I was Christian. I responded by saying that yes, I was in fact Christian. I was actually a member of The Church of Jesus Christ of Latter-day Saints.

Suddenly, her curiosity was sparked. "So, what are the rules?!" she asked me.

"The rules?" I asked with a laugh.

"Yeah. Like what rules do you follow in your church?"

I talked to her a little bit about the Word of Wisdom[5] and then got up to go see a patient when she caught my attention again.

"Hey. Wait a second!" she said in a raised voice. "I'm not done with you yet!"

Well, that took me aback! I turned to her, bewildered yet laughing.

"I have more questions!" she said. "Sit back down!"

I obediently took a seat as she continued to ask away, answering her questions here and there. By the end, she turned to me and said, "We used

---

4. Mark 12:31
5. The Word of Wisdom is a series of health guidelines we have in my church that include things like not smoking, drinking alcohol, coffee, or black tea, or doing drugs, as well as encouragement to eat healthily.

to have a lot of Christians that worked here, but now there aren't as many. It's actually quite sad. I'm glad you are a follower of Christ."

One amazing example of member missionary work in my life is my friend and colleague Mike. In the beginning, I didn't know Mike all that well. He had just moved to the area, started working with me, and came to church in my ward. But one day, Mike invited me to join some of my colleagues at his house for dinner. I accepted his invitation and when I arrived, I was surprised to find my colleagues sitting on his couch watching YouTube videos of past Conference Center performances.

"Wow. This guy is brave!" I thought. "I would never be bold enough to try that." And yet, as I watched my colleagues enjoying the Church performances and commenting on the paintings of Christ Mike had all around his house, I was inspired. When dinner was ready, he turned to me and said, "Ashley, will you bless the food" I immediately obliged. My colleagues were all in and smiling as they bowed their heads. It was so cool.

Later, Mike became good friends with me and my roommate. My roommate was not a member of the Church but she was also Christian, and she and Mike and I shared our testimonies with one another and had many uplifting conversations about God. One day, as Mike was getting ready to leave our house, he turned to my roommate and said, "Would you mind if we said a prayer before I leave?" My roommate excitedly agreed. After Mike was done praying, he said, "Next time, it's Ashley's turn!"

Through these experiences, God has shown me how heartwarming sharing the gospel can be if we just ask Him for some opportunities. I know at times it can seem scary to say this prayer because you're afraid that God will make you randomly talk to a stranger or someone you know, and you'll have to have an awkward conversation that leaves you flustered and begging to disappear.

I totally feel you! I've been there with that paralyzing fear, debating whether or not I should even try to utter that simple plea for an opportunity to share the gospel. But, let me clear this up. Sharing the gospel is just that—sharing the gospel. It doesn't require baptisms or conversions. It's not measured by how many people you bring to church or how many less active members you convince to come to family home evening. So the pressure is off, folks!

Instead, it can be measured by how many people you have conversations about the gospel with. The people that are prepared will come naturally. We succeed when we open our mouths and share what we believe. Whether people want to know more or not, we can rest assured that we have succeeded in doing our part as a member missionary when we can say, "I shared the gospel today." And when we say that prayer, asking for a little bit of extra help from God in our ministering efforts, we just might be able to both receive and give the best surprises imaginable.

> *Alright friends, I'm pretty sure you know what the invitation of the day is. So let's get to it. Today I want to invite you to say a prayer asking your Father in Heaven for an opportunity to share the gospel in some way, shape, or form. As you go about your day, pay attention to the opportunities He brings your way. Remember, it doesn't have to be teaching someone actual missionary lessons. You aren't required to invite someone to church or even tell them what church you go to. You aren't even required to talk. I mean teaching by example and sharing things on social media definitely count. Just open your heart and mind to sharing the truth, the hope, the love, and the beauty the gospel brings. Say that prayer and listen for answers throughout the day. God will not hesitate to deliver. I mean this is His work and glory, so I kind of doubt He'll randomly decide to hold out on you. You got this! I totally believe in you!*

28

War Room

"And it came to pass that after I, Nephi, had been in the land of Bountiful for the space of many days, the voice of the Lord came unto me, saying: Arise, and get thee into the mountain. And it came to pass that I arose and went up into the mountain, and cried unto the Lord." (1 Nephi 17:7)[1]

A few years ago, I watched the movie *War Room*,[2] which recounts the story of the Jordan family—a husband and wife and their teenage daughter who are struggling in their family relationships as well as their relationship with the divine. In the movie, Elizabeth Jordan, the mother in the family, meets Miss Clara, a client of hers hoping to sell her house. While touring her house, Miss Clara shows Elizabeth what she calls her "War Room"—a special closet she has dedicated to prayer and communion with the Lord. Her simple explanation is, "In order to stand up and fight the enemy, you need to get on your knees and pray."

The idea of a "War Room" has stuck with me through the years. I think we can all agree that life is a war. There are bad influences coming

---

1. Book of Mormon
2. *War Room*, directed by Alex Kendrick, written by Alex Kendrick and Stephen Kendrick, released Aug. 28, 2015.

at us from all directions as we try to stay true to the goodness of God. The adversary is smart and tactful, and he has a knack for knowing the best things to catch our attention, bring us down, and distract us from what's most important. I know. It stinks, doesn't it? So, with this idea in the back of my mind, my brain started trying to create an action plan—a revolutionary strategy to help me come out victorious in the fight to endure to the end in the gospel of Jesus Christ. And that's how I came to have my "War Rooms."

Now, I actually have two "War Rooms" in my house. I'm kind of embarrassed to admit this, but the first one is my bathroom. I guess one day I made the realization that the bathroom was the one place I knew I would have time to sit and think for a minute or so multiple times each day. That realization led me on a brainstorm to take some control over what I was going to sit and think about. I mean, that doesn't sound too weird, right?

One day, I came across a couple of scriptures that I especially liked while I was studying the Bible. I ended up writing those scriptures down in pretty colors on flashcards from my old unused college collection and then taping them to the wall right in front of where I would sit and think in the bathroom, if you know what I mean.

Now, I guess I should tell you, I don't have a private bathroom. I share it with one of my roommates. She also shares my love for Jesus, so I didn't think she would mind. The next day, I woke up and walked into the bathroom to sit and think for a bit, of course, and what was my surprise, when I saw a post-it note taped next to my flashcard on the wall. On it, my sweet roommate had written a deep question about the scripture I had posted. That started a back-and-forth discussion that continued throughout the day. It was exciting that my "War Room" efforts were affecting more people than just me.

Over time, my scripture wall grew. When I became intrigued by a scripture, I wrote it down in bright colorful pens, sometimes even doodling a little picture to accompany it, and pasted it on the wall along with inspiring quotes from one of my favorite authors. Each day, as I had the opportunity to sit and think for a bit in my new makeshift "War Room," I would lose myself in reading through these scriptures over and over and over again until they were written in my heart and mind and I could pull them out of my back pocket easier than my cell phone and car keys. It was amazing. I felt like I was being armed with truth that I could now take with me from my "War Room" out into the worldly fight.

My other "War Room" just so happens to be my closet. I know, not really all that mind-blowing or creative. But let me just tell you. My closet is pretty puny. I have to crawl in behind my hanging dresses and find a decent spot to sit each time I decide to enter, which is hopefully every day. And I try to make it cozy by bringing in pillows and blankets to ensure my cramped body is not begging to escape after five minutes of being all squished up and sitting on the hardwood floor.

While my other "War Room" has been deemed my "Scripture Wall Room," this "War Room" is different. I call it my "Escape Room" or my "Hide and Seek Room." It is where I go to escape and hide from the world—to quarantine, detox, whatever you want to call it, because the world is such a dangerous place! There are so many negative messages, harmful lies, time-wasting distractions, and toxic propagandas that slip into our minds before we can even think about putting on any personal protective equipment. The struggle is real!

So every day I throw in the towel on the world for a bit, turn off all of the lights in my room, and crawl into my closet, making sure to shut the door behind me. I leave every worldly thing outside. My phone is especially off limits! Though I may set a timer on it and leave it outside the door, just so I don't completely lose track of time if there's some appointment I have to get to or something. And then I just close my eyes and sit and breathe. I have escaped from the world and she has absolutely no idea! I've slipped away unnoticed. She will never find me! It's kind of exciting!

As I sit there and breathe, I try to erase the things of the world from my mind and connect with my spirit and heart—the old soul inside me that has seen so much more than I can remember. When thoughts pop in, I try to brush them away. Sometimes it's hard and sometimes it's not so hard. Sometimes I let them stay for a while and sometimes I just try to refocus as fast as I can.

Then, after five minutes or so, I start talking to my Family in Heaven. Sometimes I talk to my Heavenly Father; other times, it's my Heavenly Brother; and there are also times I talk to my Heavenly Mother. I tell them what's going on. I speak to them like I'm a child who just got home from school and my parents are asking me how my day went, what I learned, and what I did with my friends. I let it all out.

I relate my concerns, my worries, and my fears. I ask them questions. I ask for guidance. I ask if there's something I should be doing that I'm not, or if there's something I am doing that I shouldn't be. And then when my dialogue is over, I sit in silence again, breathing, and listening—listening for answers, for wisdom, for whisperings. And every time, the Spirit envelopes me like I'm a caterpillar in a cocoon. I go in my closet to hide from the world and each and every single time, I am sought after and found by God. And the world remains clueless! I must say, I'd like to keep it that way.

I go into my "Escape Room," my "Hide and Seek Room," or my closet "War Room" not to fight but to be conquered by love, to have my heart and soul replenished with truth, to feel sweet communion with my Creator and Maker so I can emerge that much more whole and strong and true to the woman I promised to be before I was sent here to earth. I go in there a humble caterpillar, feeling pretty jaded, numb, discouraged, or distraught, and I emerge a resurrected butterfly full of hope and life and faith and love, ready to take on the war-torn world and all it imposes. It is the sweetest, most refreshing thing I've ever experienced. It's like a makeshift private temple away from the temple.[3] And I consider it to be a holy place.

So, next time the world is getting you down, next time you feel jaded, numb, discouraged, or distraught, maybe let your brain start playing with the idea of a "War Room" or maybe even two. A place where you can go to arm yourself with truth or connect with your sweet spirit and your loving God—a place where you can go to escape from the world and detox from its lies and distractions and fake alibis, and just sit and breathe and feel and commune.

---

3. Members of The Church of Jesus Christ of Latter-day Saints go to special buildings called temples to make promises with God and get married and sealed together for eternity.

What's your War Room? Do you have one already? Or are you needing to find one? Or two? Or maybe three? Because believe me! The War Room Department is not one-size fits all. You've got a multitude of options at your fingertips. This week I want you to find and spend some time in your War Room. Take the time to ponder the scriptures, to slip away and hide from the world and connect with your soul and your loving Heavenly Family. Tell them everything! Like a little kid coming home from school. Take the time to laugh, to cry, to grin, to vent, and take the time to listen. I mean, you can't just be a taker in a relationship, so give Them Their time of day to add Their two cents to the conversation too. As you do this, I can promise you that slowly but surely, you will feel the Spirit enveloping you like a cocoon and emerge from your escape a new creature in Christ, and boy am I excited for you!

29

Faith Over Fear

---

*"Thou comest to me with a sword, and with a spear,
and with a shield: but I come to thee in the name of
the Lord of hosts, the God of the armies of Israel."
(1 Samuel 17:45)*

Have you ever been faced with a big challenge in your life that literally scares you to death? I definitely have. I had one of those moments during the beginning stages of the crazy COVID-19 pandemic. As a nurse working on an inpatient hospital unit at a major hospital in the country, talk of COVID was all around.

At first, I was under the impression that my unit would not be getting any patients who were infected with the deadly coronavirus. But one day everything changed when our manager told my colleagues and I that we would definitely be getting COVID patients and we began to clear out our unit for them. I was sent to be trained on all of the personal protective equipment and how to use it correctly and then it started to hit me how real this was.

I have always prided myself in being brave and adventurous and not scaring easily. I mean I was always the one saving my missionary companions from bugs and frogs as they screamed and hid behind chairs. But for some reason that day, after hearing all of my colleagues talking about their anxieties and worries and fears, it seemed like my courage kind of snapped like a toothpick and I was like, "How did I get myself into this?!" I felt like a soldier being deployed to the front lines of one hectic, crazy, out-of-nowhere war and suddenly all of the training I got in boot camp seemed useless and inapplicable.

I went home that day absolutely terrified of what was coming. I reached out to friends for support and that seemed to help a little, but the looming fear of imminent danger was still coming at me full speed ahead. Finally I sat down in bed, a hot mess, and began to read a devotional book by one of my favorite Christian authors—Stephanie May Wilson.

In the chapter I read, Stephanie described an experience she had snorkeling in the aquarium. She related that as she attempted to have fun and enjoy the scene of the fish swimming beneath her, her muscles were clenched tight and her legs kept sinking down as she struggled to keep herself afloat. The struggle was real and she was on the brink of calling it quits, giving up, and abandoning ship. But at that instant, the aquarium guide swam up to her, tapped her on the shoulder and explained that she just had to relax, because if she relaxed, her body would float. The more she tensed up, on the other hand, the faster she would sink.

In her devotional, Stephanie went on to compare her experience with what it's like to follow God in our lives. She stated:

> When we follow God with our lives it's only a matter of time before we find ourselves in a situation that feels foreign, bigger than us, and intimidating, forcing us to face our fears and requiring more of us than we think we have to give. In situations like these, I think we have two choices: We can go into them tense, trying to keep ourselves afloat on our own, thrashing as we try to maintain control of our surroundings and our lives . . . or, we can go into these situations having taken a deep breath, relaxing consciously and purposefully, and reminding ourselves that God has this. He is with us; He's in control, and He's taking care of us. When we thrash, we sink; but when we relax, we float.[1]

This passage hit me like a light bulb moment from heaven, and I knew it was no coincidence. Everything she said fit so perfectly with how

---

1. Stephanie May Wilson, *The Lipstick Gospel Devotional: 90 Days of Saying Yes to a God Who Is Anything But Boring* (Anthem Workshop LLC, 2017).

I was feeling. I immediately got on my knees to pray and, as tears poured down my cheeks, I asked God to forgive me for being so "tense," for not trusting Him, for letting my fear overcome my faith. I asked Him to help me relax, to help me "float," and to help me trust He had this.

Now, I won't say my fears disappeared completely, though that definitely would have been nice. But those words of wisdom helped alleviate a large portion of them and I was able to gather more hope than ever that God had a plan for me in all this messy chaos and would be able to use me for good as I took His hand and stepped into the unknown, trusting He would never lead me astray.

Over the next few months, I was thrust into chaos. My world turned upside down in a split second. My job transformed into something I never could have imagined. I mean, in nursing school, I guess I must have slept through the class on how to carry yourself through a pandemic as a frontline health-care provider, because I don't recall any pandemic-specific training or any of my professors being like, "Hey! Just a heads up! Your first year out as a nurse, the world just might be hit with a deadly virus that will kill hundreds of thousands, and we're counting on you to keep everything under control, ok? You got this! Go get 'em!"

As the chaos ensued, I was sent all over the hospital to train people on how to use protective equipment, to ensure people were using protective equipment properly, to work as a nurse on other units that needed more staff, to help care for COVID patients, to help transport COVID patients, and the list goes on. Every day I went to work having absolutely no idea where I was going or what the shift held for me until I got my assignment.

To say I was stressed is an understatement, but each day I had to remind myself to relax. "God's got this!" I told myself. "He needs you here right now. He knows He's doing. He's not going to call it quits or give up on you. He won't abandon ship or fall asleep at the wheel. If He's got this then you got this, because you are on His team and He knows He can trust you."

Soon enough I was able to relate more than ever before to the prophet Nephi when he said, "I was led by the Spirit, not knowing beforehand the things which I should do. Nevertheless, I went forth."[2]

---

2. 1 Nephi 4:6–7, Book of Mormon

Looking back, some of my sweetest work memories and greatest learning moments happened during that period of utter chaos in the center of that scary storm.

I have memories of sitting and talking with my colleagues as we waited for another COVID patient to require transportation from the Emergency Room to imaging or another unit. We became so much closer as we bonded together in the trials we shared. God needed us there that night so we could connect as a team and feel a little less alone.

I remember starting to feel like more of an equal with doctors as they listened intently to my direction on how to put on and take off protective equipment and spoke with me casually about music they liked or how their shift was going. God needed me there to boost my confidence in my ability to interact with people I had once been totally intimidated by.

I remember one night while working on a COVID unit, my sweet patient told me how much he wanted a creamy strawberry-flavored protein shake, but when I looked in the fridge, all we had were the chocolate and vanilla ones as well as one strawberry juice-flavored one with no creaminess whatsoever. Rather than going back empty-handed, however, I decided to get creative.

I took the strawberry juice and some vanilla ice cream and mixed them together good and then brought the homemade protein milkshake to his room. The joy that lit up my patient's face as he took his first sip and his repeated comments of "This is delicious! Thank you so much!" will forever stay with me. I ended up writing my homemade recipe down in his chart so that all the other nurses who cared for him later would know how to make the secret concoction. God needed me there that night to light up this sick, lonely, secluded man's life with a sweet creamy protein-filled strawberry milkshake.

Another morning after a long night at work, I headed out to where I had parked my car in a neighborhood by the hospital (because free parking rocks, right?). As I was walking, I spotted a woman and what appeared to be her two young daughters, sitting on their porch holding a sign. When I got nearer, they began clapping and I saw that their homemade sign was a tribute, thanking all the frontline healthcare providers for their service. That sweet gesture made my day after an exhausting shift at work.

I later realized that I had gone a block too far in my walk to my car, and it was only because of that mistake that I had run into this cute family, but I knew it was no mistake. God wanted me there that day so I could feel the genuine appreciation of the people in the community I was serving as I worked to protect them from the danger that surrounded us.

These sweet memories left me feeling brave and strong and proud of how far I had come as God helped me relax in the jumble of chaos and trust I was exactly where He wanted and needed me. They helped me realize that I had more to give than I thought and as long as I partnered with God, He would carry me through the storm.

Now, I am sure many of you who are facing scary predicaments in life right now are probably so tired of hearing the phrase, "Faith over fear! Faith over fear!" repeated endlessly, as if it's that easy to choose to keep faith locked in your handbag and chuck fear in the dumpster. I am sure by now you're thinking, "Hasn't anyone come up with a better quick fix solution for the daunting tasks or terrifying situations in life since the ancient times already?" And while I can't say I've found the secret recipe for eliminating fear in the blink of an eye, I honestly don't really think that's the point.

If you stop and think about it, fear is what makes you strong. If you weren't scared of anything, life would be dull and boring. You'd never find anything to make you proud of yourself or feel a need to have God in your life. If I hadn't been so terrified of facing this virulent pandemic, I would never have connected with God or felt His sweet presence in the memories I created.

I don't think it was ever in God's plan to knock fear completely out of the ballpark. Instead, I learned that all He's asking is we find the faith to float—to relax a little more, to shake out those tense muscles we have as they brace for ensuing chaos and to take a few deep breaths, trusting that God's got this, and that He needs us here right now.

Although we may not know exactly what we're doing or where He's taking us, He knows what He's doing, and He's not going to call it quits or give up on us. He won't abandon ship or fall asleep at the wheel. If He's got this then we've got this, because we are on His team, and He knows He can trust us.

Are you facing any scary or stressful predicaments in life these days? Do you feel at times that God's requiring more of you than you have to give? If not, that's wonderful, but I think most of us can say there are some things going on in life that bring at least a tinge of fear or stress into our hearts if it's not a massive rock slide. Wherever you're at today, I want you to tell God about it. Talk to Him. Have a heart to heart. Ask Him to forgive you for the "tense muscles" that are panicking and trying to put up a fight and to help you relax and float in His plan for you right now, to trust that He needs you where you are even if it is scary or uncomfortable or frustrating or annoying. Ask Him to help you create those sweet memories in the chaos that will leave you feeling brave and strong and proud of how far you've come, and I guess I'll add a passionate, "You got this! Go get 'em!"

30

My Partner in Comfort

---

*"But when the Comforter is come, whom I will send
unto you from the Father, even the Spirit of truth,
which proceedeth from the Father, he shall testify of me."*
(John 15:26)

As I mentioned, when I was young I struggled with health issues—seizures to be exact, that seemed to happen whenever I was particularly stressed. They were scary experiences that came on suddenly. They made me feel like I was floating away from this world and would never be able to come back—like separation from my family and friends and everything I loved was imminent. Pretty much, like I was about to die. The best way I can describe them is feeling like you're undergoing anesthesia and you'll never wake up. Yeah. Scary, right?

Whenever these sensations started coming on, I would yell out and ask someone to hold my hand. That seemed to ground me and give me a feeling of peace, as if holding someone's hand meant that I could trust someone had me tight in their grasp and wouldn't let me float away, disappear, or pass on. When someone was holding my hand, I generally didn't pass out. But when that lack of companionship and support was there, I could bet on losing consciousness, falling, and probably hurting myself in the process.

The worst time for seizures generally came around final exams—that period of time that all students hate, when you are bombarded with a multitude of study guides, review sessions, and stress beyond anything you've ever experienced. That stress was a bigtime trigger. I would be studying for an exam when suddenly, I would feel a seizure coming on. The seizure would happen, I'd have to lie down and sleep for a bit, and when I woke up, I would have forgotten everything I had just studied. Like legit, everything. And so, I'd have to sit back down and start from scratch studying through the same material again until I suddenly would feel another seizure coming on, and BOOM! The cycle would repeat itself again and again. It was the absolute worst!

When people talk about how much they miss high school or wish they could go back, my brain raises its eyebrows and gives a short laugh. "Yeah right?!" it seems to say. "I cannot believe you just said that!" In other words, I do not miss high school at all, because of everything I experienced then. Like zero relatability! Nada!

But it was also during that time that God showed up for me in the most undeniable ways. I remember one day during high school finals I was undergoing this horrendous cycle of stress, studying, seizures, amnesia, stress, studying, seizures, amnesia. I must have just woken up from a seizure and was feeling absolutely down in the dumps—worthless, useless, and completely overwhelmed. It was at that point that I did the only thing I had ever been taught to do during hard times. I knelt down and said a prayer begging my Heavenly Father to see me, to feel me, and to help a daughter out.

After these heartfelt pleadings, I collapsed onto my bed, reached over to my nightstand, grabbed my scriptures, and opened them—with a secret hope that somehow God would answer my prayer. I turned to the Bible Dictionary and looked up the only thing I could think of asking for at that time—"Comforter." The first scriptural reference that popped up under that was John 14:16–27, so I turned to that and started reading:

> *And I will pray the Father, and he shall give you another Comforter, that he may abide with you for ever;*
> *. . . for he dwelleth with you, and shall be in you.*
> *I will not leave you comfortless; I will come to you.*
> *. . . But the Comforter, which is the Holy Ghost, whom the Father will send in my name, **he shall teach you all things, and***

bring all things to your remembrance, *whatsoever I have said unto you.*

Peace I leave with you, my peace I give unto you*: not as the world giveth, give I unto you.* ***Let not your heart be troubled, neither let it be afraid.***

As I read that, I sat there, somewhat dumbfounded, not sure if what had just happened had really just happened. I read it again and again. It was the clearest message from God I had ever received in my teenage lifetime. God saw me. He knew me. He felt me. And He loved me. He would be with me through these painful cycles. He would send me a Comforter to "teach [me] all things, and bring all things to [my] remembrance." I did not have to let my heart be troubled or afraid. God had me and would send His Spirit to hold my hand and be, maybe not so much my "Partner in Crime," but more like my "Partner in Comfort." That was the exact personal message my heart needed at that moment to be comforted at such a crazy time.

Over the years, my seizures have become well controlled. I haven't had a seizure for ten years now. (Knock on wood.) But that one experience has stuck with me through it all and has been a driving factor in my faith and hope and love for God. My "Partner in Comfort" has journeyed with me through thick and thin and, let me tell you, the Spirit is way more than some cool travel buddy. It is a gift from God that comes to my aid whenever I need peace, ideas, or guidance. It gives me warnings of imminent danger to help me choose the path of least difficulty and most long-term happiness, and bring me comfort and peace through the obstacles of life.

Honestly, since we don't know what the Spirit looks like, I kind of picture it as a puppy. Now, before you start laughing at me, think about it for a sec! If you're anything like me, puppies are warm and fluffy and help me feel absolutely mind-blowingly amazing when I get the chance to cuddle with one. Their cuddles are the epitome of comfort, at least to me. They help me forget my sorrows for a sec and just soak in a peaceful, fun, feel-good experience. Why do you think universities bring puppies onto campus for stressed out students during finals week? Why are service dogs allowed to go visit sick people at the hospital? Point made. And, on top of that, puppies are also pretty good at warning you of imminent danger—little loyal guard dogs committed to our protection and well-being. Are you feeling me now?

So, with my loyal "Partner in Comfort" that God has given me walking beside me through life, I kind of feel on top of the world. That's not to say my life is obstacle-free, but I am pretty sure that without this Gift, life would be a lot more difficult and chaotic.

My "Partner in Comfort" was there for me when I was trying to decide what I wanted to major in in college, whether or not I should move from Utah to Maryland, and if it was the right time to buy a house. It was there for me when I was a missionary trying to share the gospel with people who just didn't seem all that interested, when I questioned what I knew was true, and when I struggled with difficult mission companions.

It was there for me when I was a new nurse feeling imposter syndrome like no other and struggling to stay put together during a worldwide pandemic. It's been there for me when I've been hit with rejection and loneliness in the dating game as I try to make the most of my single life. It has told me my worth, showered me with love when I least expected it, warned me of undesirable obstacles, and encouraged me to keep going even when life is tough. And, to tell you the truth, because God has a sense of humor, the Comforter definitely has one too. And for that, I am grateful.

One of my more memorable interactions with my "Partner in Comfort" actually came when I was a nursing student doing clinical shifts at a rehab center. So, a word of caution to those who shrink when bodily functions are discussed—just cover your ears for a minute, but it is too good to not share.

I was walking down the hall one morning at the rehab facility where my classmates and I had a clinical shift, when I suddenly received a random yet distinct impression that I had to stop. I must say, I was downright confused, but I heeded the impression. Right after I had stopped, my classmate, who was walking in front of me with a patient whom she had just helped bathe, called out to me, "Ashley! Watch out!" she said, pointing at the ground. I looked down to where she was pointing. There on the ground, about a foot from where I had been prompted to stop, was what looked like something you should hopefully see in the toilet every day. Oh. You had to ask, didn't you? Yes. I'm talking about #2.

Our wonderful patient had been seated in one of those special bathroom wheelchairs that you can put over the toilet and had decided to have a bowel movement while being wheeled down the hall. I looked up at her and said, with a smile of relief on my face, something along the lines of, "Girlfriend! You did that on purpose didn't you?! You knew I was walking behind you and just wanted me to get my white shoes dirty, didn't you?!"

My patient had had a stroke and couldn't really talk, but let me tell you, she erupted into the biggest fit of laughter I have ever heard in my life! So big that I couldn't help but laugh myself, but inside I was also laughing with relief. And all I could think was, "Wow, God! You've really got my back, don't you? Thanks a million for sending the Spirit to save me!"

I'm pretty sure that without my "Partner in Comfort," I would not have been spiritually in-tune enough to have received that prompting. So, a word of advice: heed the gut promptings you get, even when they seem like the most random, out-of-nowhere pieces of advice in the world. It will pay off!

Life isn't easy, and there will be times when it seems like undesirable obstacles are constantly showing up in our way. Life is pretty much an obstacle course, but as we rely on our "Partner in Comfort" and follow His promptings, we can be assured that we will make it out alright. Okay, all of you who were covering your ears, you can uncover them now. The nasty stuff is over. But you definitely missed out!

What have been your interactions with your "Partner in Comfort?"—someone also referred to as the Spirit, the Holy Ghost, the Comforter, or even your gut. Has God used this Gift to communicate with you? Have you showed Him that you are open to hearing from your divine travel buddy through life? Or have you been kind of distracted by the collection of easily distractible things that pop up constantly in our lives each day? If so, no shame. I get distracted all the time. It's the worst!

Today, I want you to take some time to reflect on a spiritual experience you have had with your "Partner in Comfort." Recognize how God has showed up for you in loving, caring, meaningful, or maybe even humorous ways using this sweet Messenger. Pray and thank Him for sending support when you most needed it, and ask Him to help you live worthily to keep this amazing companion by your side as you walk through the obstacle course of life.

Recommended Reading

- *The Lipstick Gospel Devotional: 90 Days of Saying Yes to a God Who is Anything But Boring* – Stephanie May Wilson (2017)

- *The Well-Watered Woman: Rooted in Truth, Growing in Grace, Flourishing in Faith* – Gretchen Saffles (2021)

- *Wildly Optimistic: Gaining New Perspectives for Life's Challenges* – Al Carraway (2019)

- *You are More Than Enough: You are Magnificent* – Ganel-Lyn Condie (2018)

- *Cheerful Christianity: A Child's Journey to Finding Jesus* – Olivia Ruth Barney (2021)

- *For the Love: Fighting for Grace in a World of Impossible Standards* – Jen Hatmaker (2015)

- *Better Than Happy: Connecting with Divinity Through Conscious Thinking* – Jody Moore (2021)

- *Silent Souls Weeping: Depression—Sharing Stories, Finding Hope* – Jane Clayson Johnson (2018)

- *Love Boldly: Embracing Your LGBTQ Loved Ones and Your Faith* – Becky Mackintosh (2019)

Acknowledgments

I am incredibly grateful to have been surrounded by such a supportive network of family and friends throughout the process of writing this book. Without their love, encouragement, and unwavering belief in me, this project would not have come to fruition.

First and foremost, I want to express my deepest gratitude to my parents. Their unconditional love, guidance, and constant encouragement have shaped me into the person I am today. They have always been my biggest cheerleaders, and I am forever grateful for their support. Thank you, Dad, for enthusiastically reading each and every chapter of this book as they came out and editing and providing feedback. And thank you, Mom, for your encouragement through the writing process and for believing in me from the beginning. Your support has meant the world. I couldn't have done it without you both.

To my dearest friends, who have stood by my side through the highs and lows of life, thank you for always being there for me and always believing in me. Your friendship has been a source of strength and inspiration. You have provided the necessary sounding boards and the comforting words during moments of self-doubt. Your belief in my abilities and your constant support have been invaluable. Your presence has made this journey more beautiful, and I am forever grateful to have you in my life.

I want to extend a special thank you to Karina Kerr Negus, whose insightful feedback and constructive criticism have played a pivotal role in shaping the ideas and concepts in this book. Your keen eye for detail and your commitment to helping me produce the best possible work have been truly invaluable.

To Suzanne Calton, thank you for being my constant source of motivation. Your infectious enthusiasm and firm belief in my abilities have pushed me to strive for greatness. Your words of encouragement have often been the much-needed catalyst that propelled me forward during times of self-doubt.

To Bookie Longe, Katie Richards, Aastha Paneru, and Elina Chun, your friendship has been a beacon of light throughout this journey. Thank you for volunteering to be the first readers of my book. Your steadfast support, insightful conversations, and willingness to lend a listening ear and provide sincere feedback have made all the difference. Your friendship has been a constant reminder of the power of connection and has fueled my creativity.

I would also like to thank my writing agent and friend, Dennis Schleicher, for his unwavering support and patience. Your belief in me has been a constant source of inspiration and your friendship has brought immeasurable joy to my life. I am truly grateful that God found a way to bring us together when I most needed you. Without you, this book would not have been possible.

Lastly, I want to express my deepest gratitude to all the readers and supporters of this book. Your encouragement and interest in my work have been a tremendous source of motivation. Thank you for embarking on this journey with me.

In writing this book, I have been fortunate to have an incredible support system. To my parents, friends, and readers, thank you for your unwavering love, encouragement, and belief in me. Your contributions have made this book possible, and I am forever grateful.

With heartfelt thanks,

Ashley

About the Author

Ashley Dyer is a Christian (Latter-day Saint) nurse, life coach, writer, blogger, speaker, and social media influencer. She is a spiritual mentor and a big advocate for mental and spiritual health as she shares uplifting messages for women of faith on Instagram. A frequently invited public speaker, she has given numerous devotionals on topics ranging from scripture study and faith crises, to Christian dating and embracing God's plan during times of uncertainty. Some of her favorite roles include best friend and cheerleader. She loves giving pep talks and finding ways to lift where she stands in her community. This is her first book.

Scan the QR Code to
follow Ashley on Instagram

BRING LIGHT
INTO YOUR LIFE

Books, Products, and Courses at:
www.cedarfort.com

Scan the QR Code to try our app
and get 3 months free!

SAVE ON
YOUR NEXT ORDER

15%
OFF

WHEN YOU USE
DISCOUNT CODE:

SAVE15